Best Garden Plants

for

Texas

Leslie Halleck • Don Williamson

Lone Pine Publishing International

The Publisher: Lone Pine Publishing
1808 B Street NW, Suite 140
Auburn, WA, USA 98001
Website: www.lonepinepublishing.com

Library and Archives Canada Cataloguing in Publication

Halleck, Leslie.
  Best garden plants for Texas / Leslie Halleck, Don Williamson.
  pages : color illustrations ; cm

Includes index.
ISBN: 978-976-650-058-4

1. Plants, Ornamental—Texas. 2. Gardening—Texas. I. Williamson, Don, 1962– II. Title.

SB453.2.T4   H35 2016   635.9/09764

Photography: All photos by Laura Peters, Tamara Eder and Tim Matheson except Aleksandra Szywala 12a,; Allison Penko 10b, 61a, 67a, 93a, 95a&b, 115b, 124b, 147b, 149a&b, 152b, 154b, 158a, 166a, 172a; Bailey Nurseries 121b; Chicagoland Grows Inc. 98b; Curtis Clark/Wikimedia 150b; Debra Knapke, 167a; Derek Fell 10a, 22, 38a&b, 46b, 50a, 56, 75, 76a, 77a, 99a&b, 100, 102a&b, 111, 113a&b, 115a, 117a, 118, 125, 131a, 132a, 133a, 146a, 161a&b; Don Williamson 10c, 126a&b; Erika Flatt 14b; Joan de Grey 20b; Kim O'Leary 12b, 24a, 26a&b, 43b, 73a&b, 87b, 124a; Janet Loughrey 133b; Joseph Scianna 153b; Leslie Halleck 20a, 34, 41, 51, 57, 63, 65a, 74a&b, 86a, 92, 96, 97a&b, 108a&b, 130a&b; Liz Klose 152a, 156a, 164a&b; furie/Flickr 129; Malcolm Manners/Flickr 103, 109a&b; Marilyn McAra 65b, 122a&b; Mark Turner 121a, 159b; Pam Beck 165a&b; PPA 59; Peter Thompstone 21a; Robert Ritchie 39b, 91a, 139a; Sandra Bit 85a; Saxon Holt 19a&b, 68a&b, 71a&b, 76b, 82b, 90a&b, 131b, 132b, 146b, 151a&b, 153a; Staci Jenkins 105b; Steve Baskauf 160a&b; Texas Cooperative 105a; Tim Wood 119a; Valleybrook Gardens 52a, 167b; Wikimedia Commons 150a; William Adams 101.

PC: P35

Table of Contents

Introduction

Starting a garden can seem like a daunting task, but it's also an exciting and rewarding adventure. This book is intended to give both beginner gardeners and new Texas residents the information they need to start planning and planting gardens of their own. It includes a wide variety of plants and provides basic plant descriptions, planting and growing information and tips for use. With this book in hand, you can begin to create a beautiful and functional landscape.

The sheer size of Texas means variations in climate and soil make it difficult to provide a singular description of growing conditions in the state. There are three main climatic zones: the semi-arid steppe climate of northern Texas, including the Panhandle; the subtropical humid climate of eastern and southern parts of the state; and the near-arid desert climate of southwestern and western Texas. Conditions can vary, however, across all of these regions.

In general, summers are hot and dry; winters are mild and short, with the coldest conditions found in the Panhandle. All of Texas will experience killing frosts, but they are rare in southern areas. Most precipitation takes place in spring and fall, with periods of drought occurring in both summer and winter. Supplemental watering is typically required through summer, though local water restrictions often dictate frequency.

The soil varies greatly in Texas. Soils are typically alkaline in central and western areas of the state and acidic in eastern and southeastern areas. Coastal areas have sandy soils; northern areas have heavier clay soils; central Texas has clay soils with a limestone base; western areas have a mixture of clay and sandy soils.

Hardiness zones and frost dates are two terms often used when discussing climate and gardening. Hardiness zones are based on minimum winter temperatures. The USDA hardiness zones in Texas range from zone 6 in the Panhandle to zone 10 in the southernmost part of the state. Plants are rated according to the zones in which they grow successfully. The average last frost date in spring combined with the first frost date in fall allows us to predict the length of the growing season and gives us an idea of when we can begin planting. Frost-free day averages range from 156 at the north of the Panhandle to 346 at the southern tip of the state.

Microclimates are small areas that are generally warmer or colder than the surrounding area. Buildings, fences, trees and other large structures can provide shelter in winter but may trap heat in summer, thus creating a warmer microclimate. The bottoms of hills are usually colder than the tops but may not be as windy. Take advantage of these areas when you plan your garden and choose your plants; you may even successfully grow out-of-zone plants in a warm, sheltered location.

Getting Started

When planning your garden, start with a quick analysis of the garden as it is now. Plants have specific requirements, and it is best to put the right plant in the right place rather than try to change your garden conditions to suit the plants you want.

Knowing which parts of your garden receive the most and least amounts of sunlight will help you choose the proper plants and decide where to plant them. Light is classified into four basic groups: full sun (direct, unobstructed light all or most of the day); partial shade (direct sun for about half the day and shade for the rest); light shade (shade all or most of the day with some sun filtering through to ground level); and full shade (no direct sunlight). Most plants prefer a specific amount of light, but many can adapt to a range of light levels.

Soil is the foundation of a garden. Plants use the soil to hold themselves upright and rely on the many resources it contains: air, water, nutrients, organic matter and a host of microbes. The soil particle size influences the amount of air, water and nutrients the

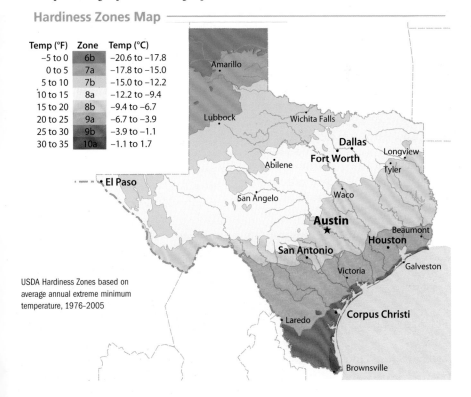

Hardiness Zones Map

Temp (°F)	Zone	Temp (°C)
–5 to 0	6b	–20.6 to –17.8
0 to 5	7a	–17.8 to –15.0
5 to 10	7b	–15.0 to –12.2
10 to 15	8a	–12.2 to –9.4
15 to 20	8b	–9.4 to –6.7
20 to 25	9a	–6.7 to –3.9
25 to 30	9b	–3.9 to –1.1
30 to 35	10a	–1.1 to 1.7

USDA Hardiness Zones based on average annual extreme minimum temperature, 1976–2005

Amarillo

Lubbock

Wichita Falls

Dallas

Fort Worth

Longview

Abilene

Tyler

El Paso

San Angelo

Waco

Austin ★

Beaumont

Houston

San Antonio

Victoria

Galveston

Corpus Christi

Laredo

Brownsville

soil can hold. Sand, with the largest particles, has lots of air space, and water and nutrients drain quickly. Clay, with the smallest particles, is high in nutrients but has very little air space. Water is therefore slow to penetrate clay and slow to drain from it.

Soil acidity or alkalinity (measured on the pH scale) influences the amount and type of nutrients available to plants. A pH of 7 is neutral; a lower pH is more acidic. Most plants prefer soil with a pH of 5.5–7.5. Soil testing kits are available at most garden centers, and soil samples can be sent to testing facilities for a more thorough analysis.

Compost is one of the best and most important amendments you can add to any type of soil. Compost improves soil by adding organic matter and nutrients, introducing soil microbes, increasing water retention and nutrient-holding capacity, and improving drainage. Adding compost is the easiest way to help correct pH extremes. You can purchase compost, or you can make it in your own backyard.

Purchasing Plants

It's important to purchase healthy plants that are free of pests and diseases. Such plants will establish quickly in your garden and will not introduce problems that may spread to other plants. You should have a good idea of what the plant is supposed to look like—its habit and the color and shape of its leaves—and then inspect the plant for signs of disease or insect damage before buying it.

The majority of plants are grown in containers. This method is an efficient way for nurseries and greenhouses to grow plants, but when plants grow in a restricted space for too long, they can become pot bound, with their roots densely encircling the inside of the pot. Avoid purchasing plants in this condition; they are often stressed and can take longer to establish. It is often possible to temporarily remove the pot to check the roots. You can look for soil-borne insects and rotten roots at the same time.

Planting Basics

The following tips apply to all plants.

- Prepare the garden before planting. Remove weeds, work in any needed amendments and loosen soil in preparation for planting if you are starting a new landscape. The prepared area should be the size of the plant's mature root system. If the soil is heavy and sticky after a rainfall, wait until it dries out and becomes crumbly again before working it. Try to plant before forecasted rain to take advantage of natural watering.

- Unwrap the roots. Remove any container to give the roots the chance to spread out naturally when planted. In particular, you should remove plastic containers, fiber pots, wire and burlap before planting trees. Fiber pots decompose very slowly, if at all, and they wick moisture away

1. Gently remove container.

2. Ensure proper planting depth.

3. Backfill with amended soil.

from the plant. Plastic and synthetic burlap don't decompose, and wire will eventually strangle the roots as they mature. The peat pots and pellets used to start annuals decompose more readily and can be planted with tender transplants. Even peat pots should be sliced down the sides, and any part of the pot that is exposed above ground should be removed to prevent water from being wicked away from the roots.

- Accommodate the rootball. As a general rule, the planting hole should be two times the width of the rootball but no deeper than its height. The top surface of the rootball should be level with the surrounding soil.

- Settle the soil with water. Good contact between the roots and the soil is important, but if you press the soil down too firmly, as often happens when you step on it, you can cause compaction. This reduces the movement of water through the soil and leaves very few air spaces. Instead, pour water in as you fill the hole with soil. The water will settle the soil evenly without allowing it to compact.

- Know the mature size of your plants. Space your plants based on how big they will grow rather than how big they are when you plant them. Large plants should have enough room to mature without interfering with walls, roof overhangs, power lines, walkways and surrounding plants.

- Identify your plants. Keep track of what's what in your garden by putting a tag next to each plant when you plant it. A gardening journal is also a great place to list the names and locations of your plants. It is very easy, for beginning and seasoned gardeners alike, to forget exactly what they planted and where they planted it.

- Water deeply. It's better to water deeply only when necessary than to water lightly more often. Deep, infrequent watering forces roots to grow as they search for water and helps them survive dry spells when water bans may restrict your watering regimen. Always check the rootzone before you water; more gardeners over water than under water. Mulch helps retain moisture and is a must-have in Texas. Container gardens are the watering exception and may need watering every day during heat waves.

Choosing Plants

Features such as decorative fruit, variegated or colorful leaves and interesting bark provide visual appeal when plants aren't blooming. When choosing your plants, aim for a variety of sizes, shapes, textures, bloom times and other features. A well-planned garden will captivate your attention year-round.

Annuals

Annuals are newly planted each year and are only expected to last for a single growing season. Their flowers and decorative

4. Settle backfilled soil with water.

5. Water the plant well.

6. Add a layer of mulch.

foliage provide bright splashes of color and can fill in spaces around immature trees, shrubs and perennials.

Annuals are easy to plant and are usually sold in cell-packs of four or six plants, 4-inch pots or quart-sized containers. The roots quickly fill the space in these small pots, so be sure to loosen the rootball before planting. Run your thumb up each side to break up the roots.

Many annuals are easily grown from seed and can be started directly in the garden once the soil has begun to warm up.

Perennials

Perennials grow for three or more years. They usually die back to the ground each fall and send up new shoots in spring, though they can also be evergreen or semi-shrubby. They often have a shorter period of bloom than annuals but require less care.

Many perennials benefit from being divided every few years. Dividing keeps them growing and blooming vigorously, and in some cases controls their spread. It involves digging the plant up, removing dead debris, breaking the plant into several pieces and replanting some or all of the pieces. Extras can be shared with fellow gardeners. A good rule of thumb is to divide spring-blooming perennials in fall and fall-blooming plants in spring.

Trees & Shrubs

Trees and shrubs provide the bones of the garden. They are often the slowest growing plants but usually live the longest. Characterized by leaf type, they may be deciduous or evergreen, and needled or broad-leaved. Here in Texas, trees are crucial to providing shade. Trees can make time spent outdoors more enjoyable, cut energy costs and, along with shrubs, provide urban wildlife habitat.

Trees should have as little disturbed soil as possible at the bottom of the planting hole. Loose dirt settles over time, and sinking even an inch can kill some trees. The prepared area for trees and shrubs should be two to four times wider than the rootball.

Staking is not typically recommended for trees; however, in high wind situations, it can be beneficial for newly planted specimens. Stakes support the rootball until it grows enough to support the tree; they should allow the trunk to move with the wind and should only remain in place for up to one year.

Annuals and perennials in a mixed border

Trees and shrubs provide interest year-round.

Annual pruning can improve blooming for flowering trees and shrubs; others need only be pruned to remove dead or diseased wood. If you plan to keep a formal hedge, be sure to select plants that tolerate regular shearing.

Roses

Roses are beautiful shrubs with lovely, often fragrant blooms. Traditionally, most roses bloomed once in spring or offered a repeat flush of blooms in fall. Some newer varieties will bloom from spring until first frost. Repeat-blooming roses should be deadheaded to encourage more flower production. Spent flowers of one-time bloomers can be left in place for the colorful hips that develop.

Generally, roses prefer a fertile soil with good drainage. Add plenty of compost or other organic matter to the soil before planting. Add expanded shale to improve drainage in heavier clay soils. Keep the roots well watered during the growing season. Many roses are quite durable and will adapt to poorer conditions. Texas Earth-Kind® roses require little care to perform well in most Texas landscapes.

Roses, like all shrubs, have specific pruning requirements. Consult with your local extension department or garden center for specific information pertaining to your roses.

Roses are lovely on their own or in mixed borders.

Virginia creeper provides beautiful red fall color.

Vines

Vines or climbing plants are useful for screening and shade, especially in a location too small for a tree. They may be woody or herbaceous and annual or perennial. Vines may cling to surfaces, have wrapping tendrils or stems or need to be tied in place with string.

Sturdy trellises, arbors, porch railings, fences, obelisks, pergolas, walls, poles and trees are all possible vine supports. Choose a support that is suitable for the vine you are growing, and ensure it's in place before you plant to avoid disturbing the roots later.

Bulbs, Corms & Tubers

These plants have fleshy, underground storage organs that allow them to survive extended periods of dormancy. They are often grown for the bright splashes of color their flowers provide. They may flower in spring, summer or fall. Each one has an ideal depth and time of year at which to plant.

Hardy bulbs can be left in the ground and will flower every year. Tender bulbs, corms and tubers are generally dug up in fall, stored in a cool, frost-free location over winter and replanted in spring. Some bulbs require

Crinum lilies bloom throughout the summer.

a chilling period to produce flowers; in Texas, these bulbs must be pre-chilled prior to planting each year because most areas remain too warm through winter.

Herbs

Herbs are plants with medicinal or culinary purposes. A few common culinary herbs are included in this book. Even if you don't cook with herbs, the often-fragrant foliage adds its aroma to the garden, and the plants can be quite decorative in form, leaf and flower.

Many herbs have pollen-producing flowers that attract butterflies, bees and humming-birds. They also attract predatory insects, which feast on problem insects such as aphids, mealybugs and whiteflies.

Chives excel in sheltered, well-drained areas.

Ornamental grasses add color, variety and texture.

Grasses, Ferns & Groundcovers

Many plants are grown for their decorative foliage rather than their flowers. Ornamental grasses, ferns, groundcovers and other foliage plants add a variety of colors, textures and forms to the garden.

Ornamental grasses and grass-like plants provide interest throughout the year, even winter if the withered blades are left to stand until spring rather than cutting them back in fall. Divide them when the clumps begin to die out in the center.

Ferns provide a lacy foliage accent and combine attractively with broad-leaved perennials and shrubs. Ferns usually prefer moist, shady gardens, but some selections thrive with a bit of direct sun.

Plants used for groundcovers are often vigorous, spreading or procumbent. These types of plants are frequently used as an alternative to grass, as a living mulch around the base of other, taller plants, to prevent erosion or purely for decorative purposes.

A Final Comment

The more you discover about the fascinating world of plants—whether from reading books, talking to other gardeners, admiring the creative designs of others or experimenting with something new in your own garden—the more rewarding your gardening experience will be. This book is intended as a guide to germinate and nurture your passion for plants and to help you acclimate to your new Texas garden.

Angelonia
Angelonia

A. angustifolia (above & below)

With its loose, airy spikes of orchid-like flowers, angelonia makes a welcome addition to any garden.

Growing

Angelonia prefers **full sun** but tolerates some afternoon shade. The soil should be **fertile, moist** and **well drained**. Although this plant grows naturally in damp areas, such as along ditches and near ponds, it is fairly drought tolerant. Plant out after the chance of frost has passed.

Tips

Added to an annual or mixed border, angelonia looks most attractive when planted in groups. It is also well suited to a pondside or streamside planting.

Also called: angel wings, summer snapdragon
Features: attractive purple, blue, pink, white or bicolored flowers **Height:** 12–24" **Spread:** 12"

Recommended

A. angustifolia is a bushy, upright plant with loose spikes of flowers in varied shades of purple. Cultivars with white or bicolored flowers are available, including **Angelface Series, Angelmist Series** and **Serena Series**, which is a Texas Superstar® plant.

The individual flowers look a bit like orchid blossoms, but angelonia is actually in the same family as snapdragons.

Begonia

Begonia

With their beautiful flowers, compact habit and decorative foliage, begonias are one of the best plants for brightening up a shady garden.

Growing

Light shade or **partial shade** is best for these plants, though some wax begonias tolerate sun if their soil is kept moist. The soil should be **fertile, rich in organic matter, neutral to acidic** and **well drained**. Allow the soil to dry out slightly between waterings.

Begonias love warm weather, so don't plant them out before the soil warms in spring. If they sit in cold soil, they may become stunted and fail to thrive.

Tips

All begonias are useful for shaded garden beds and planters. Wax begonias have a neat, rounded habit that makes them particularly attractive as edging plants. Wax begonias are easy-care compact bedding plants, while the larger Dragon Wing™ begonias are perfect for containers.

B. × hybrida 'Dragon Wing' (above), B. semperflorens (below)

Wax begonias are ideal flowers for the time-strapped gardener because they are generally pest free, and they bloom all summer, even without deadheading.

Recommended

B. × hybrida **Dragon Wing**™ begonias offer excellent garden performance under many conditions. They tolerate both sun and shade. Their pendulous growth habit makes them perfect for containers and baskets. **Baby Wing**™ begonias offer up the same performance on a compact scale.

B. semperflorens (wax begonias) have pink, white, red or bicolored flowers and green, bronze, reddish or white-variegated foliage.

Features: pink, white, red, orange or bicolored flowers; decorative foliage **Height:** 6–24" **Spread:** 6–24"

Celosia

Celosia

The unusual, wrinkled texture of the celosia's flowers and the incredible variety of flower forms make them a showstopper in any garden.

Growing

Celosia prefers **full sun** and is tolerant of excessive heat. The soil should be **fertile** and **well drained** with plenty of organic material worked in. Celosia likes to be watered regularly.

Celosia is a self-cleaning annual, so it does not require deadheading. A plant that has its first flower bloom pinched out will be fuller and bear many more flowers than a plant that has not been pinched.

Tips

Use celosia in borders and beds as well as in planters. The flowers make interesting additions to cut arrangements, either fresh or dried. A mass planting of plume celosia looks bright and cheerful in the garden.

Recommended

C. argentea is the species from which both crested and plume-type cultivars have been developed. The species itself is never grown.

C. cristata (crested celosia) has blooms that resemble brains or rooster combs. This group has many varieties and cultivars in bright, vivid colors.

C. plumosa (plume celosia) has feathery, plume-like blooms. This group also has many varieties and cultivars in deep, rich colors. 'New Look' is a variety particularly well-suited to Texas.

Features: red, orange, gold, yellow, pink or purple flowers **Height:** 10–36" **Spread:** 10–36"

C. spicata 'Flamingo' (above), C. cristata (below)

C. spicata (spiked cockscomb, wheat celosia) produces narrow, spiky flower heads, reminiscent of heads of wheat. Unlike *C. argentea*, spiked cockscomb produces numerous flowers, with an almost shrubby look, in more muted colors. Cultivars are available.

The popular crested varieties make excellent cut flowers.

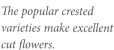

Cigar Plant
Cuphea

C. ignea (above), *C. llavea* (below)

The unique blooms of cigar plant make them perfect as border plants in high traffic areas of the landscape or in containers. This plant never fails to generate a plethora of compliments, which gardeners always appreciate.

Growing

Cigar plant prefers **full sun** or **partial shade** in **moderately fertile, well-drained** soil. It does best with regular watering but can handle short periods of dryness.

This wonderful plant attracts hummingbirds and butterflies to your garden.

Tips

Cigar plant is an excellent plant for containers of all descriptions. It is also effective in an annual or mixed border and as an edging plant.

Recommended

C. hyssopifolia (Mexican heather, false heather, elfin herb) is a bushy, much-branched plant that forms a flat-topped mound 12–24" tall and slightly wider than the height. The flowers have green calyces and light purple, pink or, sometimes, white petals.

C. ignea (*C. platycentra*; cigar flower, firecracker plant) is a spreading, freely branching plant 12–24" tall and 12–36" wide. The common names relate to the thin, tubular, bright red-orange flowers.

C. llavea (bat-face cuphea, St. Peter plant, tiny mice) is a mounding to spreading plant 12–18" tall and 12–24" wide. It produces an abundance of flowers with green to violet calyces and bright red petals. The two longest stamens give the flower the appearance of the face of a bat or mouse.

Also called: cigar flower **Features:** unique, colorful flowers; habit **Height:** 6–24" **Spread:** 10–36"

Cleome

Cleome

C. hassleriana (above & below)

Create a bold and exotic display in your garden with these lovely, unusual flowers.

Growing

Cleomes prefer **full sun** but tolerate late-afternoon shade. Plants adapt to most soils, though mixing in **organic matter** to help retain water is a good idea. These plants are drought tolerant but perform best when watered regularly.

Pinch out the tip of the center stem on young plants to encourage branching and more blooms. Deadhead to prolong blooming.

Tips

Cleomes can be planted in groups at the back of a border or in the center of an island bed. These striking plants also make an attractive addition to a large mixed container planting.

Also called: spider flower **Features:** attractive, scented foliage; colorful flowers
Height: 2–5' **Spread:** 2–3'

Recommended

C. × hybrid 'Senorita Rosalita' from Proven Winners is a heat tolerant, thornless and dense-growing hybrid cleome. This cultivar does not require deadheading and blooms continuously until first frost. The foliage has a purple tinge. The flowers are lavender-pink and sterile, so you won't have to worry about re-seeding. It grows 2–4' tall.

Many other cultivars are also available.

Cleome attracts hummingbirds and provides them with nectar well into fall because the flowers keep on blooming after many other plants have finished for the year.

Coleus
Solenostemon (Coleus)

S. scutellarioides mixed cultivars (above & below)

There is a coleus for everyone. With foliage from brash yellows, oranges and reds to deep maroon and rose selections, coleus has colors, textures and variations that are almost limitless.

Growing

Coleus prefers to grow in **light shade** or **partial shade**, but it tolerates full shade if the shade isn't too dense or full sun if the plants are watered regularly. The soil should be of **average to rich fertility, humus rich, moist** and **well drained**.

Place the seeds in a refrigerator for one or two days before planting them on the soil surface; the cold assists in breaking the seeds' dormancy. The seeds also need light to germinate. Seedlings are green at first, but leaf variegation develops as the plants mature.

When flower buds develop, it is best to pinch them off, because the plants tend to stretch out and become less attractive after they flower.

Tips

The bold, colorful foliage makes a dramatic impact when the plants are grouped together as edging plants or in beds, borders or mixed containers. Coleus can also be grown indoors as a houseplant in a bright room.

Recommended

S. scutellarioides (*Coleus blumei* var. *verschaffeltii*) forms a bushy mound of foliage. The leaf edges range from slightly toothed to very ruffled. The leaves are usually multi-colored with shades ranging from pale greenish yellow to deep purple-black. Dozens of cultivars are available, but many cannot be started from seed.

Many new sun-tolerant varieties, which are vegetatively propagated, are available.

Features: brightly colored foliage; light purple, insignificant flowers **Height:** 6–36" **Spread:** usually equal to height

Cosmos

Cosmos

C. sulphureus (above), *C. bipinnatus* (below)

Cosmos is a low-cost, low-maintenance, cottage-garden flower that is easy to grow and never fails to delight. It can handle the toughest, hottest, driest conditions.

Growing

Cosmos likes **full sun** and soil of **average fertility** that is **well drained**. Over-fertilizing and overwatering can reduce the number of flowers. Deadhead to encourage more flowers.

Plant out transplants or direct sow the seeds into warm soil after the last frost. Cosmos often self-seeds.

Tips

Cosmos looks attractive in cottage gardens, in borders or mass planted in informal beds. A second sowing in midsummer provides a colorful fall show.

Features: gold, orange, yellow, scarlet, white, pink or magenta flowers; attractive foliage; easy to grow **Height:** 12–36" **Spread:** 12–24"

Recommended

C. bipinnatus is taller growing with large, white, pink or magenta blooms. **Sonata Series** and **'Seashells'** are popular varieties.

C. sulphureus (yellow cosmos) is an erect, dense plant that bears gold, orange, scarlet or yellow flowers.

The name cosmos is from the Greek kosmos, meaning "good order" or "harmony."

Dusty Miller
Senecio

'Silver Dust' (above), S. cineraria (below)

Dusty miller is a great addition to cool season planters, window boxes and mixed borders where the deeply lobed, soft, silvery gray foliage makes a good backdrop for the brightly colored flowers of other annuals.

Growing

Dusty miller grows well in **full sun** or **partial shade**. The soil should be of **average fertility** and **well drained**. Pinch off the flowers before they bloom. They aren't showy, and they use energy that would otherwise go to producing more foliage.

A wonderful filler for fresh- or dried-flower arrangements, dusty miller adds a lacy texture.

Tips

Dusty miller is a subshrub that can behave as a short-lived perennial in Texas gardens, but we most often use dusty miller as a cool-season annual. The soft, lacy, silvery foliage of this plant is its main feature. Dusty miller is used primarily as an edging plant but also in beds, borders and containers.

Recommended

S. cineraria forms a mound of fuzzy, silvery gray foliage that is lobed or finely divided. Many cultivars with impressive foliage shades and shapes have been developed.

Features: silvery foliage; neat habit; yellow to cream flowers **Height:** 12–24" **Spread:** equal to height or slightly narrower

Esperanza
Tecoma

T. stans (above & below)

It's difficult not to be impressed by this prolific blooming Texas native. It blooms almost all season long, producing bright, sunny yellow, orange and almost-red flowers that emit a sweet scent. Esperanza is guaranteed to attract hummingbirds to the garden.

Growing

Esperanza thrives in **full sun**. Partial shade is tolerated in sandy sites in limestone conditions. **Fertile, moist, well-drained** soil with added **organic matter** is best, but plants can thrive equally well in heavier clay soils. Regardless of its drought tolerance, esperanza benefits from supplemental watering during long, dry spells, or flowering will come to a halt.

Tips

Esperanza can be used in mixed beds and borders as a background plant. It is especially stunning when planted with other fiery-blooming plants, or with cool-colored flowers and foliage including lantana, sun-loving coleus varieties, tropical butterfly weed and hibiscus.

Recommended

T. stans (*Bignonia stans*, *Stenolobium stans*) is an open shrub or small tree that is often grown as an annual in the cooler parts of the state. This species produces bright green foliage and funnel-shaped, lemon yellow, pendulous flowers that can reach 4" in length. The flowers emerge in spring and continue through fall. **'Gold Star'** is slightly smaller compared to the species and blooms much earlier and heavier. There are many new cultivars with orange-colored blooms.

Also called: yellow bells **Features:** bright yellow, orange or orange-red flowers; decorative foliage; shrub-like growth habit **Height:** 3–5' **Spread:** 3–4'

In warmer parts of Texas, esperanza may survive winter; plants are top hardy in zone 9 and above, and root hardy in zone 8.

Euphorbia
Euphorbia

E. graminea (above), *E. marginata* (below)

These mounding plants are admired for the bright white bracts that surround their tiny flowers. A second show of color appears in fall when the leaves turn purple, red or orange.

Growing

Euphorbia grows well in **full sun** or **light shade**, in **moist, well-drained, humus-rich** soil of **average fertility**. This plant is drought tolerant and can be invasive in fertile soil. It does not tolerate wet conditions and requires good drainage. Plant it in spring or fall.

Tips

Use euphorbia in a mixed or herbaceous borders. It is especially attractive in mixed container plantings and hanging baskets.

Recommended

E. graminea '**Diamond Frost**' is a Proven Winners award-winning annual that produces airy, white flowers in great abundance, slightly obscuring the delicate, dark green foliage. It grows 12–18" tall and 10–12" wide.

E. marginata, a native annual, is a vigorous, bushy plant that has bright green, oval leaves with clear white margins. Petal-like, white bracts surround tiny clusters of flowers in summer. '**Summer Icicle**' is a dwarf selection with variegated foliage.

You may wish to wear gloves when handling this plant, because the sap contains latex, which can irritate the skin.

Also called: ghostweed **Features:** colorful bracts; low maintenance **Height:** 12–24" **Spread:** 10–12"

Fan Flower

Scaevola

*F*an flower's intriguing, one-sided flowers add interest to hanging baskets, planters and window boxes.

Growing

Fan flower grows well in **full sun** or **light shade**. The soil should be of **average fertility, moist** and very **well drained**. Water regularly because this plant doesn't like to dry out completely. It does, however, recover quickly from wilting when watered.

Tips

Fan flower is popular for hanging baskets and containers, but it can also be used along the tops of retaining walls where it will trail down. This plant makes an interesting addition to mixed borders, or it can be used under shrubs, where the long, trailing stems form an attractive groundcover.

S. aemula (above & below)

Recommended

S. aemula forms a mound of foliage from which trailing stems emerge. The fan-shaped flowers come in shades of purple, usually with white bases. The species is rarely grown because there are many improved cultivars. **New Wonder**™ and **Surdiva Series** are excellent performers in Texas.

Given the right conditions, this Australian plant will flower abundantly from March through to frost.

Features: unique, blue or purple flowers; trailing habit
Height: up to 8" **Spread:** 36" or more

Firebush

Hamelia

H. patens

Firebush is an attractive shrub, donning summer flowers and fiery-colored fall foliage. It is a Texas Superstar® plant.

Growing

Firebush prefers **full sun** to with some late afternoon shade. Any soil will suffice as long as it is **well drained**.

Although this plant is technically a shrub, it is often grown as an annual throughout Texas.

Tips

Firebush is an ideal specimen plant, but it also mixes well with other native or non-native shrubs and trees in mixed beds and borders.

Firebush is highly sought after by butterflies, hummingbirds and a variety of other pollinating, nectar-loving insects and birds.

Recommended

H. patens is a tropical evergreen shrub that produces softly hairy foliage and an abundance of tubular, mostly red or reddish orange flowers with darker stripes. Later in the season, fruit follows the flowers, changing from green to red to purplish black. In fall, the foliage changes from the dark green displayed all summer to a variety of reddish shades. Cultivars are available.

Also called: scarlet bush, Mexican fire bush **Features:** fiery, May to November flowers; colorful fall foliage; habit **Height:** 24–36" **Spread:** 24–36"

Floss Flower

Ageratum

A. houstonianum (above & below)

The fluffy flowers, often in shades of blue, add softness and texture to the garden.

Growing

Floss flower prefers **full sun** but tolerates partial shade. The soil should be **fertile, moist** and **well drained**. A moisture-retaining mulch prevents the soil from drying out excessively.

Floss flower will have its best performance in spring and fall. Deadhead to prolong blooming and to keep plants looking tidy.

Tips

The smaller selections, which become almost completely covered in flowers, make excellent edging plants for flowerbeds and are attractive when grouped in masses or grown in planters. The taller selections can be included in the center of a flowerbed and are useful as cut flowers.

Recommended

A. hybrids produce flowers in a range of blues, violets and purples. Not all ageratums are heat-tolerant enough to perform well in Texas. But the Proven Winners **Artist Series** does well, growing only 8–12" tall in the garden and in containers. **'Blue Diamond'** is another heat tolerant hybrid with a larger growth habit, growing to 30" tall in the garden.

The genus name, Ageratum, *is from the Greek and means "without age," referring to the long-lasting flowers.*

Also called: ageratum **Features:** cool-colored, fuzzy flowers; mounded habit **Height:** 8–30" **Spread:** 6–18"

Globe Amaranth

Gomphrena

G. globosa (above & below)

Growing

Globe amaranth prefers **full sun**. The soil should be of **average fertility** and **well drained**. This plant is drought and heat tolerant and does not require much supplemental water.

Soak seeds in water for two to four days to encourage sprouting before sowing into warm soil above 70° F.

Tips

Globe amaranth can be included in informal and cottage gardens as well as mixed beds and borders. Sometimes overlooked by gardeners because it doesn't start flowering until midsummer, globe amaranth is worth including in the garden for the long-lasting color it provides from midsummer to the first frost. Some of the new hybrids are particularly showy.

The flowerheads of globe amaranth are made up of brightly colored, papery bracts from which the tiny flowers emerge. It is a Texas Superstar® plant.

Globe amaranth flowers are popular for cutting and drying. Harvest the blooms when they become round and plump; dry them upside down in a cool, dry location.

Recommended

G. globosa forms a rounded, bushy plant that grows 12–24" tall. It bears papery, clover-like flowers in shades of purple, magenta, white or pink. **'Fireworks'** is a powerhouse bloomer and a true Texas tough annual that produces an explosion of hot pink blooms tipped with bright yellow. It is excellent for low-water gardens and grows 3–4' tall.

G. haageana **'Strawberry Fields'** has a bushy growth habit with good heat and drought tolerance. Its bright red flowerheads resemble strawberries.

Features: purple, magenta, pink, white or red flowers **Height:** 12"–4' **Spread:** 8–15"

Impatiens
Impatiens

*I*mpatiens are the high-wattage darlings of the shade garden, delivering masses of flowers in a wide variety of colors.

Growing

Impatiens grow best in **partial shade** or **light shade** but tolerate full shade. The soil should be **fertile, humus rich, moist** and **well drained**.

Tips

Impatiens are known for their ability to grow and flower profusely, even in shade. Mass plant them in beds under trees, along shady fences or walls or in porch planters. They also look lovely in hanging baskets.

Recommended

I. walleriana (impatiens, busy Lizzie) flowers in shades of purple, red, burgundy, pink, yellow, salmon, orange, apricot or white and can be bicolored. Dozens of cultivars are available.

I. walleriana (above & below)

Be aware, impatiens are susceptible to downy mildew. Infected plants should be removed immediately.

Features: flowers in shades of purple, red, burgundy, pink, yellow, salmon, orange, apricot, white or bicolored; flowers well in shade **Height:** 6–36" **Spread:** 12–24"

Lantana

Lantana

L. camara 'Spreading Sunset' (above & below)

Lantana rarely suffers from any pests or diseases.

This low-maintenance plant, with its stunning flowers, thrives in hot weather and won't suffer if you forget to water it. Butterflies love this prolific bloomer.

Growing

Lantana grows best in **full sun** but tolerates some afternoon shade. The soil should be **fertile** and **well drained**, but lantana tolerates other soils. This plant is heat and drought tolerant, making it excellent for low-water and low-maintenance planting areas.

Tips

Lantana is a tender shrub that is often used as an annual. It grows quickly and makes a stunning addition to mixed planters, combining well with geraniums and other heat-tolerant annuals.

Recommended

L. camara is a bushy plant that bears round clusters of flowers in a variety of colors. The flowers often change color as they mature, giving the flower clusters a striking, multi-colored appearance. A wide variety of cultivars is available. Sterile cultivars such as **New Gold**™, a Texas Superstar® plant, as well as **'Texas Flame'** ('Dallas Red') and the **Bandana Series**, are particularly excellent performers.

L. montevidensis (weeping lantana) is a spreading shrub that produces a dense mat of coarsely toothed foliage. It bears long-stalked flower stems supporting purple-pink to purple flowers with yellow eyes. It grows 8–36" tall and 24–48" wide. It is a Texas Superstar® plant.

Features: stunning flowers in shades of yellow, orange, pink, purple, red or white, often in combination
Height: 8–36" **Spread:** up to 4'

Madagascar Periwinkle
Catharanthus

C. roseus (above & below)

Madagascar periwinkle is a forgiving annual, tolerant of dry spells, searing sun and city pollution. It exhibits grace under all sorts of pressure.

Growing

Madagascar periwinkle prefers **full sun** but tolerates partial shade. Any **well-drained** soil is fine. This plant tolerates pollution and drought but prefers to be watered regularly. It doesn't like to be too wet or too cold. Avoid planting this annual until the soil has warmed because it may fail to thrive if planted in cold or wet soil.

Tips

Madagascar periwinkle does well in the sunniest, warmest part of the garden. Plant it in a bed along an exposed driveway or against the south-facing wall of the house. It can also be used in hanging baskets, in containers and as a temporary groundcover.

Also called: flowering periwinkle **Features:** attractive foliage; flowers in shades of red, rose, pink, mauve or white, often with contrasting centers; durability **Height:** 6–24" **Spread:** usually equal to or greater than height

One of the best annuals to use in front of homes on busy streets, Madagascar periwinkle blooms happily despite exposure to exhaust fumes and dust.

Recommended

C. roseus (*Vinca rosea*) forms a mound of strong stems. The flowers are pink, red or white, often with contrasting centers. Many cultivars are available, including the **Cora Series**, which are Texas Superstar® plants and one of the first selections resistant to the *Phytophthora* fungus.

If this annual is planted in the same spot year after year, a fungus called Phytophthora *may become a problem—switch locations or grow the plant in containers if this occurs.*

Ornamental Kale
Brassica

B. oleracea (above & below)

Ornamental kale has stunning, colorful foliage and is wonderful in beds, containers and flower boxes during the cool season.

Growing
Ornamental kale prefers **full sun** but tolerates partial shade. The soil should be **neutral to slightly alkaline, fertile, moist** and **well drained**. For best results, fertilize a few times through winter.

Ornamental kale plants can be started in trays and transplanted in fall. Many packages of seeds contain a variety of cultivars. Wait until some true leaves develop before thinning. When thinning seedlings, use the discards in salads. To extend the ornamental value of ornamental kale, remove the flowers when the plant bolts.

Tips
Ornamental kale is a tough, bold plant that is at home in both vegetable gardens and flowerbeds.

Recommended
B. oleracea forms loose, erect rosettes of large, often fringed leaves in shades of purple, red, pink and white. It grows 12–24" tall, with an equal spread. **Osaka Series** plants grow 12" tall and wide, with wavy leaves that are red to pink in the center and blue to green near the edges. **'Redbor'** is a stunning deep purple/burgundy type that grows to 24" tall with ruffled foliage. **'Red Russian'** provides blue-green leaves with red to purple stems.

The plant colors brighten after a light frost or when the air temperature drops below 50° F.

Features: edible, colorful foliage **Height:** 12–24"
Spread: 12–24"

Pentas
Pentas

This plant is a welcome addition to the annual garden, not only for its pretty flowers, but also because it is both heat and drought tolerant. Pentas is a constant bloomer from spring through first frost.

Growing

Pentas grows best in **full sun**, but plants can tolerate some afternoon shade. The soil should be **fertile, moist** and **well drained**. Deadhead to encourage continuous flowering and to keep plants looking tidy. Pinch plants to encourage bushy growth.

In warmer parts of the state, zone 9 or higher, pentas can often perennialize.

Tips

Pentas makes a lovely addition to mixed or herbaceous beds and borders. The coarse, dark foliage creates a background against which brightly colored flowers stand out. It can also be grown in containers, and cuttings taken in late summer can be grown indoors over winter.

P. lanceolata 'New Look Red' (above), *P. lanceolata* (below)

Recommended

P. lanceolata is a subshrub that is grown as an annual. It has an erect or occasionally prostrate habit. Red, pink, purple or white flowers are produced in clusters. Cultivars are available, including the **New Look Series** and the **Butterfly Series**. 'Butterfly Deep Pink' is a Texas Superstar® plant.

Pentas is a tremendous butterfly and hummingbird plant.

Also called: star clusters, Egyptian star
Features: pink, red, purple or white flowers; foliage **Height:** 9–36" **Spread:** 9–36"

Persian Shield

Strobilanthes

S. dyerianus (above & below)

This plant is actually a tender shrub that is treated as an annual. It can be overwintered in a cool, bright location indoors.

This plant's iridescent foliage in metallic shades of purple, bronze, silver and pink adds a bright touch to any annual planting.

Growing
Persian shield grows well in **full shade** or **partial shade**, especially in morning sun with afternoon shade. It can be grown in full sun but wilts in the hottest part of the day even with adequate moisture. The soil should be **average to fertile, light** and very **well drained**.

Pinch the growing tips to encourage bushy growth. Cuttings can be started in late summer and overwintered indoors.

Tips
The colorful foliage provides a dramatic background in annual or mixed beds and borders and in container plantings. For stunning contrast, combine Persian shield with plants that have yellow, white, red or purple flowers.

Recommended
S. dyerianus forms a mound of silver- or purple-flushed foliage with contrasting dark green, bronze or purple veins and margins.

Features: decorative foliage; blue flowers **Height:** 18–36"
Spread: 24–36" or more

Petunia

Petunia

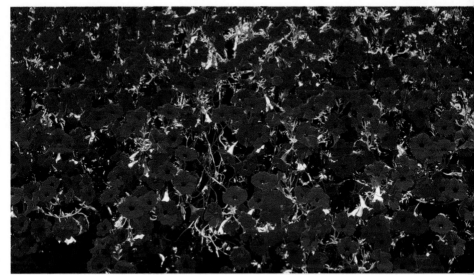

P. 'Purple Wave' (above), P. *multiflora* type (below)

For their speedy growth, prolific blooming, ease of care and huge selection, petunias are hard to beat.

Growing

Petunias prefer **full sun**. The soil should be of **average to rich fertility, light, sandy** and **well drained**. Pinch halfway back in midsummer to keep plants bushy and to encourage new growth and flowers. Petunias grow best during spring and fall in Texas.

Tips

Use petunias in beds, borders, containers and hanging baskets.

Recommended

P. × *hybrida* is a large group of popular, sun-loving annuals that fall into three categories: grandifloras have the largest flowers in the widest range of colors, but they can be damaged by rain; multifloras bear more flowers that are smaller and less easily damaged by heavy rain; and millifloras have the smallest flowers in the narrowest range of colors, but this type is the most prolific and least likely to be damaged by heavy rain. The **Tidal Wave Series** is particularly heat-tolerant and are Texas Superstar® plants.

The rekindling of interest in petunias was largely owing to the development of exciting, new selections, such as the Supertunia hybrids and Wave family of petunias. These hybrid series are heat-tolerant, continuous-blooming, vigorous-spreading, dense-growing plants that offer tremendous options for hanging baskets, containers and borders.

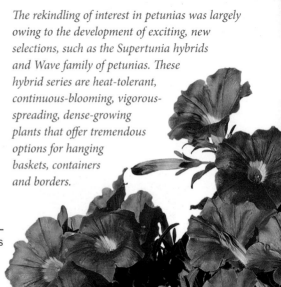

Features: colorful flowers; versatile plants
Height: 6–24" **Spread:** 12–24" or wider

Purslane

Portulaca

P. cultivars (above & below)

Purslane will spread wide, almost like a low-growing ground cover when planted in beds, but acts as a trailing plant when placed in containers or hanging baskets.

For a brilliant show in the hottest, driest, most neglected area of the garden, you can't go wrong with purslane. Purslane offers up brightly colored, teacup-shaped blooms all summer long, supported by flat, oval-shaped, succulent foliage.

Growing

Purslane requires **full sun**. It is tolerant of poor soil, as long as the soil is **well drained**. Remember to water purslane occasionally. As long as the location is sunny, this plant does well with minimal care.

Tips

Purslane grows well under the eaves of a house or in a dry, rocky, exposed area. It makes a great edging plant for retaining walls or raised beds. It also makes a great addition to a hanging basket on a sunny front porch.

Recommended

P. oleracea produces succulent foliage and single or double, neon yellow flowers. There are many cultivars available with both prostrate and mounding growth habits. The **Yubi Series** is a popular choice with a collection of colors, including apricot, red and pink. It is a Texas Superstar® plant.

Also called: portulaca, moss rose
Features: colorful, drought-resistant, summer flowers in shades of red, pink, yellow, white, purple, orange and peach
Height: 8–12" **Spread:** 12–36"

Salvia
Salvia

Salvias should be part of every annual garden—the attractive and varied forms have something to offer every style of garden. Annual salvias are excellent hummingbird plants.

Growing

All salvia plants prefer **full sun** but tolerate light shade. The soil should be **moist, well drained** and of **average to rich fertility**, with a lot of organic matter.

To keep plants producing flowers, water often and fertilize monthly.

Tips

Salvias look excellent grouped in beds and borders and in containers. The flowers are long lasting and make good cut flowers for arrangements.

Recommended

S. coccinea (hummingbird sage, scarlet sage) is a bushy, upright plant that bears whorled spikes of white, pink, blue or purple flowers. In warmer parts of the state, hummingbird sage can survive winter. **'Coral Nymph'** and **'Lady in Red'** are two excellent varieties.

S. splendens (tropical sage, scarlet sage) is grown for its spikes of bright red, tubular flowers. Recently, cultivars have become available with flowers in white, pink, purple or orange. **'Sizzler'** is an excellent recent introduction in red, while **'Wendy's Wish'** is a vigorous, tall, pink-blooming variety.

S. splendens (above), *S. coccinea* 'Coral Nymph' (below)

With over 900 species of Salvia, you're sure to find one you'll like for your garden.

Also called: sage **Features:** colorful, summer flowers; attractive foliage
Height: 16–30" **Spread:** 9–14"

Tapioca Plant
Manihot

M. esculenta 'Variegata'

Tapioca plant is a South American root crop from which tapioca is produced.

Tapioca plant is a stunning tropical foliage plant prized for its vibrant chartreuse and yellow variegated leaves.

Growing
Tapioca plant thrives in warm temperatures in a **full sun** location. Plants prefer **moist, well-drained** soil, but well-established plants are easy to care for. Fertilize regularly to maximize growth during the season.

Tips
Tapioca plants make excellent specimen or background plants for annuals and perennials. Combine them with lantana, salvia and purslane for easy-care, tropical color. They are striking feature plants in large containers.

Recommended
M. esculenta **'Variegata'** forms a fast growing, shrub-like specimen in the landscape. It is grown as an annual in most of the state but will perennialize in the southern-most parts. Tapioca plant is a Texas Superstar® plant.

Also called: bitter cassava, manioc, yuca
Features: showy, variegated foliage **Height:** 3–5'
Spread: up to 5'

Viola
Viola

V. × wittrockiana (above), *V. tricolor* (below)

Violas are planted in early fall, often blooming off and on throughout winter, and are known to put on quite the show in spring. Late-blooming forms can also be planted in late winter.

Growing
Violas prefer **full sun** but tolerate some afternoon shade. The soil should be **fertile, moist** and **well drained**. Violas do best in cool weather, so plant them in late September through winter and they'll provide you with blooms through spring.

Tips
Violas can be used in beds and borders for winter color or mixed with spring-flowering bulbs. They can also be grown in containers. With the varied color combinations available, pansies complement almost every other type of bedding plant. The dense clusters of smaller violas make excellent edging plants.

Because of the long growing season, pansies must be occasionally fertilized through winter.

Features: blue, purple, red, orange, yellow, pink, white or multi-colored flowers **Height:** 3–10" **Spread:** 6–12"

Recommended
V. tricolor (Johnny-jump-up) is a perennial grown as an annual but will reseed. It bears flowers in shades of purple, lavender, blue, white or yellow, with dark purple upper petals. The lower petals are usually streaked with dark purple. Many cultivars exist with larger flowers in various colors above heart-shaped leaves.

V. × wittrockiana (pansy) is available in a wide variety of hybrids and cultivars that have solid, patterned, bicolored and multi-colored flowers in every size imaginable with face-like markings. The foliage is bright green and lightly scalloped along the edges. The smaller flowered annual hybrids are often referred to as "violas." Trailing varieties such as '**Purple Rain**' are perfect for containers and baskets.

Wishbone Flower

Torenia

T. fournieri (above & below)

Wishbone flower produces unique blooms in shades of blue. Be sure to point them out to children, who are often intrigued by familiar shapes showing up in strange places.

Growing

Wishbone flower is a versatile plant in that it can be grown in any light from **full sun to full shade**. In sunny conditions, plants have a mounded growth habit. In full shade they act as a prostrate ground cover. The soil should be **fertile, light, humus rich** and **moist**. This plant requires regular watering.

Don't cover the seeds when planting; they require light to germinate.

Tips

Wishbone flower is very soothing and subtle because of the cool-colored blooms. It blends well in a shade garden. It can be massed in a shaded bed or border, used as an edging plant or added to mixed containers and hanging baskets.

Recommended

T. fournieri **hybrids** are vigorous and excellent for containers. The **Catalina Series** offers up unique yellow-throated blooms. The **Summer Wave Series** offers up blooms in blue, purple and violet and is outstanding in Texas gardens.

Wishbone flower gets its name from the arrangement of the stamens (male parts) in the center of the flower.

Features: attractive, interesting, purple, pink, blue, violet, burgundy, white or bicolored flowers **Height:** 4–12" (depending on sun or shade) **Spread:** up to 36"

Zinnia
Zinnia

'Profusion White' (above & below)

It's no wonder that zinnias are so popular, given their ease of care and non-stop blooms.

Growing
Zinnias grow best in **full sun**. The soil should be **fertile, rich in organic matter, moist** and **well drained**. Deadhead to prolong blooming and to keep plants looking neat.

Tips
Zinnias are useful in beds, borders and containers. The dwarf selections can be used as edging plants. These plants provide wonderful fall color and attract butterflies to the garden.

Mildew can be a problem for zinnias, so choose mildew-resistant cultivars and grow them in locations with good air circulation.

Recommended
Z. angustifolia (Mexican bush zinnia) is a low, mounding, mildew-resistant plant that bears yellow, orange or white flowers. It grows 8–16" tall. Cultivars are available in bright, vivid colors and a range of sizes.

Z. × hybrida **Profusion Series** is extremely heat and drought tolerant and has a mounding growth habit. Plants grow to 18" tall and 24" wide. They are disease tolerant with eight bloom colors. **'Orange,' 'White'** and **'Cherry'** are All-America Selections Gold Medal Winners.

Features: bushy habit; flowers in shades of red, orange, yellow, pink, red, magenta, white or bicolored
Height: 8–18" **Spread:** 12–24"

Artemisia
Artemisia

'Powis Castle' (above), *A. stelleriana* (below)

Most artemisias are valued for their silvery foliage, not their flowers. The silver foliage provides striking contrast to flowers and other foliage colors in the garden.

Growing

Artemisias grow best in **full sun**. The soil should be of **low to average fertility** and **well drained**. These plants dislike wet, humid conditions.

When artemisias begin to look straggly, cut them back hard to encourage new growth and to maintain a neater form. Divide them every year or two, when plant clumps appear to be thinning in the centers.

Some artemisias can spread and become invasive in the garden.

Tips

Use artemisias in mixed perennial borders. Their silvery gray foliage makes them good backdrop plants to use behind brightly colored flowers. They are also useful for filling in spaces between other plants. Smaller forms may be used to create knot gardens or used in containers.

Recommended

A. × **'Powis Castle'** is a mounding, shrubby plant with feathery, silvery gray foliage. Plants can quickly reach 4' in width and typically grow 24–36" tall. Prune to control size and to encourage new growth in the center of the plant.

A. schmidtiana **'Silver Mound'** is a compact grower, reaching 10–14" tall and 16–18" wide. It has bright silver, feathery foliage and makes a great edging or container plant.

A. stelleriana has deeply lobed, silvery leaves covered in felt-like hairs. The species can grow 12–18" tall and wide. Some cultivars such as **Silver Cascade®** act like trailing plants, growing only 6–8" tall and 12–14" wide.

Also called: wormwood, sage **Features:** silvery gray, feathery or deeply lobed foliage **Height:** 12–36" **Spread:** 6"–4' **Hardiness:** zones 3–8

Baptisia

Baptisia

Attractive green foliage and spikes of bright blue flowers in early summer make this native Texas plant a worthy addition to any garden.

Growing

Baptisia prefers **full sun** but tolerates partial shade, though too much shade causes lank growth that flops over easily. The soil should be of **poor to average fertility, loose** and **well drained**.

Once established, this tough perennial is unfazed by drought and heat. It resents disturbance, so it doesn't need dividing.

Tips

Baptisia can be used in an informal border or a cottage garden. It is an attractive addition for a naturalized planting, on a slope or in any sunny, well-drained spot in the garden.

'Purple Smoke' (above), *B. australis* (below)

Recommended

B. alba (white wild indigo) is an erect perennial with a bushy growth habit. It bears tall spikes of white flowers that are sometimes marked with purple. It grows 2–4' tall and 2' wide.

B. australis (false blue indigo) is an upright or somewhat spreading, clump-forming plant that bears spikes of purple-blue flowers in early summer.

B. 'Carolina Moonlight' grows 4–4½' tall and 3–4' wide. Clusters of soft yellow flowers are borne in late spring. The foliage turns to silvery blue during the hottest period of summer.

B. 'Purple Smoke' grows 4½' tall, bearing violet flowers with dark purple centers.

B. sphaerocarpa (yellow wild indigo) grows 2–3' tall and bears yellow flowers in early summer.

The lupine-like blooms are showstoppers in the garden and are great for cutting.

Also called: false indigo **Features:** late spring or early summer, purple, blue, yellow or white flowers; habit; foliage **Height:** 2–5' **Spread:** 2–4' **Hardiness:** zones 3–9

Black-Eyed Susan

Rudbeckia

R. fulgida var. sullivantii 'Goldsturm' (above & below)

The cultivar 'Goldsturm' is an excellent anchor perennial because of its long life, bright yellow flowers and long blooming season. It doesn't need division, won't die out in the center and won't encroach on its neighbors.

Growing

Black-eyed Susan grows well in **full sun** with a bit of afternoon shade. The soil should be of **average fertility** and **well drained**. Established plants are drought tolerant, but regular watering is best.

Divide if you wish in spring or fall, every three to five years. Deadhead plants to encourage new flower buds.

Tips

Black-eyed Susan is a tough, long-lived, low-maintenance perennial. Plant it wherever you want a casual look. It looks great planted in drifts with ornamental grasses. Include this native plant in wildflower and natural gardens, beds and borders.

Recommended

R. fulgida is an upright, spreading plant bearing orange-yellow flowers with brown centers. **Var.** *sullivantii* '**Goldsturm**' bears large, bright, golden yellow flowers.

R. maxima is an upright, native perennial with spoon-shaped, large, blue-green foliage and daisy-like, bright yellow flowers with very prominent conical centers that face upward. This species grows 5–6' tall and 2' wide.

Several Rudbeckia *species are touted as "claybusters" because they tolerate fairly heavy clay soils.*

Features: bright yellow, orange or red, midsummer to fall flowers with brown or green centers; attractive foliage; easy to grow **Height:** 24"–6' **Spread:** 12–24" **Hardiness:** zones 3–9

Blackfoot Daisy
Melampodium

This Texas native sports small but cheery, white, daisy-like blooms. Tidy, mounded plants bloom profusely spring through fall.

Growing
Plant blackfoot daisy in a **full sun** location. Provide **well drained** soil, as plants don't like wet feet. Provide supplemental water the first growing season until plants become established. Once established, do not overwater.

Blackfoot daisy can reseed. Shear spent flowers to encourage new blooms.

Tips
Blackfoot daisy is perfect for any low-water or xeri-scaping project. Use it in masses or as edging at the front of mixed perennial plantings, easements and walkways.

Recommended
M. leucanthum is a low, bushy, mounding perennial that blooms prolifically most of the year. Honey-scented blooms are attractive to bees and butterflies.

M. leucanthum

Features: bright white, yellow-centered, daisy-like flowers; easy to grow; low water usage **Height:** 12"
Spread: 12–24"
Hardiness: zones 5–11

Blackfoot daisy is almost maintenance-free, disease and pest resistant, and once established needs little to no supplemental water.

Blazing Star
Liatris

L. spicata 'Kobold' (above), L. spicata (below)

Blazing star is an outstanding flower with fuzzy, spiked blossoms above grass-like foliage. It is an excellent plant for attracting butterflies to the garden.

Blazing star makes an excellent cut flower.

Growing

Blazing star prefers **full sun**. The soil should be of **average fertility, loose** and **well drained.** Water well during the growing season, but don't allow the plants to stand in water during cool weather. Mulch during summer to prevent moisture loss.

Trim off the spent flower spikes to promote a longer blooming period and to keep blazing star looking tidy.

Tips

Use blazing star in mixed perennial beds and wildflower stands. Plant it in a location that has good drainage to avoid root rot in winter. Blazing star also grows well in planters.

Recommended

L. aspera (rough gayfeather) is a clump-forming, native perennial with densely clustered foliage and purple-spiked flowerheads. This species grows up to 6' tall and 12–24" wide. (Zones 4–9)

L. elegans (pinkscale gayfeather) produces similar flowers to other species but with pale white inner petals. This species grows 2–4' tall and is native to Texas. (Zones 7–9)

L. punctata (snakeroot) is a tuberous, native perennial with narrow leaves and dense, purple flowerheads. It grows up to 36" tall and 24" wide. (Zones 3–7)

L. spicata (blazing star, spiked gayfeather) is a clump-forming, erect plant. The flowers are pinkish purple or white. Several cultivars are available.

Also called: gayfeather **Features:** summer flowers; grass-like foliage **Height:** 18"–6' **Spread:** 12–24" **Hardiness:** zones 3–9

Butterfly Weed
Asclepias

Butterfly weed, a North American native, will attract a bounty of butterflies to your garden. It is a major food source for the monarch butterfly.

Growing
Butterfly weed prefers **full sun** and **well-drained** soil. It tolerates drought once established but enjoys some moisture in an extended drought. Deadhead to encourage a second blooming.

Butterfly weed is slow to start in spring. To avoid inadvertently digging it up, place a marker beside each plant in fall.

A. tuberosa (above), A. curassavica (below)

The deep taproot makes division very difficult. To propagate, use the seedlings that sprout up around the base of the plant.

Tips
Use butterfly weed in mixed perennial beds, on dry banks, in neglected areas and in wildflower, cottage and butterfly gardens.

Recommended
A. curassavica (tropical butterfly weed) is an evergreen subshrub that is often grown as an annual. It bears red or orange-red flowers, sometimes yellow or white, with tinges of yellowy orange. The foliage is proportionate to the size of the flower clusters and is smooth in texture. It grows 24–48" tall and spreads 18–24".

A. tuberosa forms a clump of upright, leafy stems. It bears clusters of vivid orange flowers from midsummer to early fall. A variety of cultivars offer solid or bicolored flowers in shades of scarlet, gold, orange or pink. It grows 12–30" tall and spreads 12–18".

Be careful not to pick off or destroy the green-and-black-striped caterpillars that feed on butterfly weed—they will become beautiful monarch butterflies.

Also called: milkweed **Features:** orange, yellow, red, pink, white or bicolored flowers; attractive form **Height:** 12–48"
Spread: 12–24" **Hardiness:** zones 3–9

Cardinal Flower
Lobelia

L. cardinalis (above & below)

The brilliant red of these native Texas flowers are irresistible to hummingbirds and also make good cut flowers.

Growing
Cardinal flowers grow well in **light shade** or **partial shade**. Morning sun with afternoon shade is best. The soil should be **fertile, slightly acidic** and **moist**. Avoid letting the soil dry out completely, especially in a sunny location.

Deadhead to keep the plants neat and to encourage a possible second flush of blooms. Mulch plants lightly in winter for protection.

Plants tend to self-seed, but seedlings may not be identical to parent plants. Seedlings can be moved to new locations, or they can be left where they are to replace the short-lived parent plants.

Tips
These plants are best suited to streamside or pondside plantings. They can also be included in moist perennial beds and borders, or in any location where they will be watered regularly.

Recommended
L. cardinalis forms an upright clump of bronze-green leaves and bears spikes of bright red flowers from summer to fall. There are also many hybrids and cultivars available, often with flowers in shades of blue, purple, red or pink. Some hybrids and cultivars are as hardy as the species, while others are less hardy.

These lovely members of the bellflower family contain deadly alkaloids that have poisoned people who tried to use the flowers in herbal medicines.

Features: bright red, purple, blue or pink, summer flowers; bronze-green foliage **Height:** 24"–4' **Spread:** 12–24" **Hardiness:** zones 4–9

Catmint

Nepeta

Catmint is an easy-to-grow perennial that provides a wonderful show of flowers summer through fall. It is an excellent foraging plant for bees.

Growing

Catmint grows well in **full sun** or light afternoon shade. The soil should be of **average fertility** and **well drained**. Plants tend to flop over in soil that is too fertile.

Pinch plants back in early summer to encourage bushy, compact growth. Cut back after blooming to encourage a second flush of flowers in fall.

Tips

The lower-growing catmints can be used to edge borders and pathways and can also be used in rock gardens. Taller selections make lovely additions to perennial beds. All catmints work well in herb gardens and with roses in cottage gardens.

Recommended

N. **'Blue Beauty'** ('Souvenir d' André Chaudron') forms an upright, spreading clump. It grows 18–36" tall and spreads about 18". The gray-green foliage is fragrant, and the large flowers are dark purple-blue.

N. × *faassenii* forms a clump of upright, spreading stems. Spikes of blue or lavender flowers are produced in spring and summer and sometimes again in fall. Many cultivars are available. **'Walker's Low'** is a particularly showy cultivar.

N. **'Six Hills Giant'** is a large, vigorous plant about 36" tall and about 24" in spread. It bears large, showy spikes of deep lavender blue flowers.

N. 'Six Hills Giant' (above), *N.* × *faassenii* (below)

*If you grow catmint, you may find that cats are drawn to your garden—this plant is related to catnip (*N.* cataria), which is well known for its attractiveness to cats.*

Features: spring or summer flowers; habit; fragrant foliage
Height: 10–36" **Spread:** 18–36" **Hardiness:** zones 3–8

Columbine

Aquilegia

A. chrysantha (above), A. canadensis (below)

Few flowers signal spring quite so singularly as columbines. Their nodding flowers and spacious foliage look light and graceful wherever you plant them. Hummingbirds are regular visitors to the flowers.

Columbines self-seed but are not invasive. The new seedlings are often a different color than the parent plants. Blame it on the bees.

Growing

Columbines grow best in **partial shade** or **light shade**. They prefer soil that is **fertile, moist** and **well drained**, but adapt well to most soil conditions. Do not overwater.

Division is not required but can be done to propagate desirable plants. The divided plants may take a while to recover because columbines dislike having their roots disturbed.

Tips

Use columbines in well-drained shade gardens, formal or casual borders and naturalized or woodland gardens. Most of the large-flowered hybrids are not well suited to Texas heat and soils.

Recommended

A. canadensis (wild columbine, Canada columbine) is a native plant that is common in woodlands and fields. It bears yellow flowers with red spurs.

A. chrysantha var. *hinckleyana* (Hinckley's golden columbine) grows 18–24" tall and 24–36" wide. It bears large, bright yellow flowers and blue-green foliage. It is a Texas Superstar® plant.

A. vulgaris (European columbine, common columbine) has been used to develop many hybrids and cultivars with flowers in a variety of colors.

Features: red, yellow, pink, purple, blue or white, spring and summer flowers; color of spurs often differs from that of petals; attractive foliage **Height:** 7–30" **Spread:** 12–36" **Hardiness:** zones 3–8

Coneflower

Echinacea

Purple coneflower is a stalwart fixture in the Texas perennial garden. Its mauve petals offset by a spiky, orange center are bountiful and irresistible to butterflies. Many new hybrid cultivars in a range of colors are also available.

Growing

Coneflower grows well in **full sun** or very light afternoon shade. It tolerates any **well-drained** soil but prefers an **average to rich** soil. The thick taproots make this plant drought resistant, but it prefers to have regular water.

Deadhead early in the season to prolong flowering. Later on, you may wish to leave the flowerheads in place to self-seed or to provide winter interest. Pinch plants back or thin out the stems in early summer to encourage bushy growth that is less prone to mildew.

Divide every four years or so in spring or fall. Most of the new colorful cultivars are shorter-lived perennials in Texas gardens.

Tips

Use coneflowers in mixed perennial beds, either in groups or as single specimens. They can also be added to wildflower stands and natural areas. The dry flowerheads make an interesting feature in fall and winter gardens.

Coneflower attracts wildlife to the garden, providing pollen, nectar and seeds to various hungry visitors.

'Magnus' and 'White Swan' (above), *E. purpurea* (below)

Recommended

E. purpurea is an upright plant that is covered in prickly hairs. It bears purple flowers with rusty orange centers. Additional varieties are available, including selections with white or pink flowers.

Many new hybrids offer an expanded color range of orange, red, yellow and peach blooms—even double flowers. **'Flame Thrower,' 'Mama Mia,' 'Secret Passion,' 'Sundown'** and **'Tiki Torch'** are good performers.

Features: midsummer to fall flowers; persistent seedheads **Height:** 2–5' **Spread:** 12–24"
Hardiness: zones 3–8

Coral Bells

Heuchera

'Palace Purple' (above), *H. sanguinea* (below)

From soft yellow-greens and oranges to midnight purples and silvery, dappled maroons, coral bells offer a great variety of foliage options for a shady perennial garden.

Growing

Coral bells grow best in **partial shade** or **light shade**. The foliage colors can bleach out in **full sun**, and plants grow leggy in very heavy shade. The soil should be of **average to rich fertility, humus rich, neutral to alkaline, moist** and **well drained**. Good air circulation is essential. Deadhead to prolong the bloom.

Coral bells have a strange habit of pushing themselves up out of the soil because of their shallow root systems. Mulch in fall if the plants begin heaving from the ground.

Every two or three years, coral bells can be divided to remove the oldest, woodiest roots and stems. Replant crown divisions at or just above soil level.

Tips

Use coral bells as edging plants in mixed perennial beds, in clusters in woodland gardens or as groundcovers in low-traffic areas. Combine different foliage types for an interesting display. All varieties make excellent container plants.

Recommended

These days, there is a bounty of beautiful cultivars available with almost limitless variations of foliage markings and colors. A few top performers include 'Georgia Peach,' 'Lime Rickey,' 'Obsidian,' 'Palace Purple' and 'Peach Flambé,' but there are many more to choose from.

Also called: alum root **Features:** very decorative foliage; spring or summer flowers **Height:** 2–4' **Spread:** 6–18" **Hardiness:** zones 3–9

Daylily
Hemerocallis

'Dewey Roquemore' (above), 'Bonanza' (below)

The daylily's adaptability and durability combined with its seemingly endless variety in color, blooming period, size and texture make them a garden favorite.

Growing

Daylily grows in varied light conditions from **full sun to light shade**. Take care not to plant in heavy shade, as flowers will be few and far between. The soil should be **fertile, moist** and **well drained**, but these plants adapt to most conditions and are Texas tough once established.

Deadhead to prolong the blooming period. Be careful when deadheading purple-flowered daylilies because the sap can stain fingers and clothes.

Divide every two or three years to keep plants vigorous and to propagate them. The plants can, however, be left indefinitely without dividing.

Tips

Plant daylilies alone, or group them in mixed perennial beds, on banks and in ditches to control erosion. They can be naturalized in woodland or meadow gardens. Small varieties are also nice in planters.

Recommended

Daylilies come in an almost infinite number of forms, sizes and colors in a range of species, cultivars and hybrids. Visit your local garden center or daylily grower to find out what is available and most suitable for your garden.

All parts of the daylily are edible. The flowers are the sweetest and tastiest part of the plant and can be eaten both raw and cooked.

Features: spring and summer flowers in every color except blue and pure white; grass-like foliage
Height: 1–4' **Spread:** 1–4' **Hardiness:** zones 2–8

Dianthus

Dianthus

D. chinensis (above), D. gratianopolitanus (below)

The many varieties of dianthus mean that in Texas, they are both popular, easy-to-grow perennials as well as seasonal ornamentals for fall and winter.

Growing

Dianthus prefers **full sun** but tolerates some afternoon shade. The soil should be **neutral to alkaline** and **well-drained**. These plants hate to stand in water. Established plants are very drought tolerant.

While some *Dianthus* species are long-lived, low-maintenance perennials, others are short-lived perennials or biennials, so in most of Texas, they are frequently used as cool-season annuals, planted in fall. If you choose to perennialize them in the garden, they will typically stop blooming in the heat of summer. In August, shear off the tops to encourage fresh fall blooms.

Tips

Use cheddar pink in mixed perennial beds, on rock and retaining walls, for edging borders and walkways, in cutting gardens and even as groundcovers. Combine China pink with other cool season annuals such as pansies and dusty miller. It is excellent for containers.

Recommended

D. chinensis (China pink) is a clumping, short-lived perennial usually grown as an annual. It bears sturdy, white, red, pink, magenta or multi-colored blooms. Many cultivars are available, ranging from dwarf plants to 36" tall specimens. The **Ideal Series** is commonly available. The newer **Parfait Series** offers up compact plants with very large, stunning, multi-colored flowers.

D. gratianopolitanus (cheddar pink) is long-lived and forms a very dense, spreading mat of 4–8" tall, evergreen, silvery gray foliage with sweet-scented flowers, usually in shades of pink. **'Bath's Pink'** can reach 10" tall, has blue-green foliage and bears an abundance of light to medium pink flowers. **'Firewitch'** ('Feuerhexe') is an upright selection that bears rosy pink flowers.

Many Dianthus *varieties produce wonderfully sweet fragrances. They attract butterflies to the garden.*

Also called: pink **Features:** pink, red, white, purple or multi-colored, spring or summer flowers; attractive foliage **Height:** 4–36" **Spread:** 6–24" **Hardiness:** zones 3–9

Flame Acanthus
Anisacanthus

A. quadrifidus var. *wrightii*

The fiery orange to red blooms of this Texas native brighten up any garden, even in light shade.

Growing

Flame acanthus is an easy to grow, drought tolerant heat lover that can be grown in **full sun** or **partial shade**. The soil should be **poor** and **well drained**.

Plants are bushy and will spread. Shear plants, or even cut them back hard periodically to keep flame acanthus blooming.

Also called: hummingbird bush **Features:** orange to red, midsummer to fall flowers; attractive flaky bark **Height:** 3–5' **Spread:** 3–5' **Hardiness:** top hardy zones 8–9; root hardy to zone 7

Tips

Flame acanthus has an informal look. It can be used to fill in large swaths of less-tended garden spaces, or used in mixed perennial beds. It can even be used as a small hedge.

Recommended

A. quadrifidus var. *wrightii* is a small, shrubby perennial that produces tubular, orange to red flowers midsummer through fall, followed by small capsule fruit. Plants become semi-woody, and the flaky bark is attractive in winter. Foliage emerges late in spring, and plants start blooming midsummer.

This showy but tough perennial will help hummingbirds zero in on your garden from midsummer through fall.

Hardy Hibiscus
Hibiscus

H. moscheutos cultivars (above & below)

Hardy hibiscus towers over most other perennials in the garden and puts on quite a show. Although the extremely large flowers last only a single day, hardy hibiscus stands up to the abuse of a hot Texas summer.

Growing

Grow hardy hibiscus in **full sun**. The soil should be **humus rich, moist** and **well drained**. Hardy hibiscus is a heavy feeder and benefits from a side dressing of fertilizer when it begins to leaf out.

If a quick freeze follows a wet fall, hardy hibiscus may die out.

Divide in spring. Prune by one-half in June for bushier, more compact growth. Deadhead to keep the plant tidy. If you cut your hardy hibiscus back in fall, be sure to mark its location because this plant is slow to emerge in spring.

Tips

This plant adds interest to the back of an informal mixed perennial bed and attracts hummingbirds. The large flowers create a bold focal point in late-summer gardens.

Recommended

H. moscheutos is a large, vigorous plant with strong stems. The huge flowers can be up to 12" across. Cultivars are available, including some wonderful plants like '**Cranberry Punch**,' bearing deep reddish pink blossoms. '**Lord Baltimore**' and '**Moy Grande**' are Texas Superstar® plants.

Also called: rose mallow **Features:** white, red or pink, midsummer to frost flowers **Height:** 18"–8' **Spread:** 36" **Hardiness:** zones 4–9

Hosta

Hosta

'Francee' (above), *H.* hybrid (below)

While hostas grown in Texas typically fail to rival the vigor and size of those grown in more northern climates, they can still be a good option for a moist shade garden. Certain varieties are more heat tolerant than others.

Growing

Hostas prefer **light shade** or **partial shade** but will grow in full shade. Morning sun and afternoon shade is best; afternoon sun will scorch hostas. The soil should be **fertile, moist** and **well drained**, but most soils are tolerated. Hostas are fairly drought tolerant once established, especially if given a mulch to help them retain moisture.

Division is not required but can be done every few years in spring or summer to propagate new plants.

Also called: plantain lily **Features:** decorative foliage; summer and fall flowers **Height:** 4–36" **Spread:** 6"–4' **Hardiness:** zones 3–8

Tips

Hostas make wonderful woodland plants and look very attractive when combined with ferns and other fine-textured plants. Hostas are also good plants for a mixed border, particularly when used to hide the ugly, leggy, lower stems and branches of some shrubs.

Recommended

Hostas have been subjected to a great deal of crossbreeding and hybridizing, resulting in hundreds of cultivars. Visit your local garden center for the best suited varieties. **'Blue Angel,' 'Francee,' 'Patriot,' 'So Sweet,' 'Sugar and Cream'** and **'Sum and Substance'** are top performers in our heat.

Hostas' dense growth and thick, shade-providing leaves allow them to suppress weeds.

Lamb's Ears

Stachys

'Big Ears' (above), *S. byzantina* (below)

Named for their soft, fuzzy leaves, lamb's ears have silvery foliage that beautifully contrasts with any bold-colored plants that are near them, and they will soften hard lines and surfaces.

Growing

Lamb's ears grow best in **full sun**. The soil should be of **poor to average fertility** and **well drained**. The leaves can rot in humid weather if the soil is poorly drained. Remove spent flower spikes to keep the plants looking neat.

Many plants in the mint family contain antibacterial and antifungal compounds. When lamb's ears is used as a poultice on wounds, it may actually encourage healing.

Tips

Lamb's ears make a great groundcover in a new garden where the soil has not yet been amended. When used to edge borders and pathways, they provide a soft, silvery backdrop for more vibrant colors. For a silvery accent, plant a small group of lamb's ears in a border.

Recommended

S. byzantina forms a mat of thick, woolly rosettes of leaves. Pinkish purple flowers bloom in early summer. The species can be quite invasive, so choosing a cultivar may be wise. The many cultivars offer a variety of foliage colors, sizes and flowers. **'Big Ears'** ('Countesse Helen von Stein') is a clump-forming perennial that produces fuzzy leaves twice as large as those of other species or cultivars.

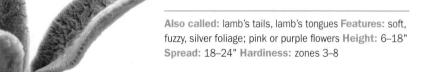

Also called: lamb's tails, lamb's tongues **Features:** soft, fuzzy, silver foliage; pink or purple flowers **Height:** 6–18" **Spread:** 18–24" **Hardiness:** zones 3–8

Lenten Rose

Helleborus

Don't let its beauty fool you: Lenten rose is one of our toughest and most versatile Texas perennials. This hardy evergreen shade bloomer tolerates heavy soils and blooms fall through spring, when most other plants are dormant.

Growing

Lenten roses prefer **light shade** or **full shade**. They do tolerate some direct morning sun if the soil stays evenly moist. The soil should be **fertile, humus rich, neutral to alkaline, moist** and **well drained**. However, plants typically thrive even in heavy clay soils and dry shade.

Tips

Use these plants in mixed shade beds or naturalize them in a woodland garden. They also perform very well in containers.

Recommended

H. argutifolius (Corsican Lenten rose) **'Silver Lace'** has gorgeous silver foliage and white to greenish flowers.

H. niger (Christmas rose) has flowers with pink buds that open to white with a greenish center. **'Josef Lemper'** is an excellent variety.

H. orientalis (above & below)

H. orientalis (Lenten rose) is a clump-forming, evergreen perennial. It grows 12–24" tall, with an equal spread. It bears white or greenish flowers that turn pink as they mature in mid- or late spring. There are many new hybrid cultivars that offer up a range of bloom colors. **'Blue Lady,' 'Cinnamon Snow,' 'Ivory Prince,' 'Red Lady'** and many other beautiful hybrids are available.

All parts of Lenten rose are toxic, and the leaf edges can be sharp, so wear long sleeves and gloves when planting or dividing these plants.

Also called: Christmas rose **Features:** late fall to mid-spring flowers **Height:** 12–24" **Spread:** 12–24" **Hardiness:** zones 4–9

Mexican Mint Marigold
Tagetes

T. lucida

This fall-blooming perennial is often used as a substitute for French tarragon. The bright yellow blooms attract migrating butterflies and bring life to the fall garden.

Growing

Plant Mexican mint marigold in a **full sun** location. It can be grown in a variety of soils, including poor, as long as the soil is **well drained**. Water regularly until this plant is established; then reduce to weekly watering.

Mexican mint marigold plants will die to the ground in a hard freeze, but re-emerge the following spring. Divide Mexican mint marigold by digging and splitting the clumps every several years.

Marigolds are edible; add the leaves to soups, salad dressings and teas.

Tips

A native of Mexico and the southwestern U.S., Mexican mint marigold is both drought and heat tolerant. It will naturalize and spread freely. Include it in your herb garden.

Recommended

T. lucida is a semi-woody sub-shrub that forms clumps that bear clusters of small, yellow flower heads. The narrow, dark green leaves have a fragrance and flavor similar to anise or licorice.

Features: small, yellow, fall through early winter flowers; edible, scented foliage **Height:** 24–36"
Spread: 24–36" **Hardiness:** zones 8–11

Mexican Petunia

Ruellia

R. brittoniana

Dwarf forms of Mexican petunia make tidy and compact clumps that produce a bounty of purple, pink or white blooms, which attract butterflies from early summer through frost.

Growing

Mexican petunia blooms best in a **full sun** location; it will tolerate shade but produce fewer blooms. It is tolerant of a variety of soils and drainage conditions. While drought tolerant once established, Mexican petunia performs better with irrigation during the hottest months. It responds well to fertilizers that contain higher levels of phosphorus.

Plants are often evergreen, but after a hard freeze, they may go dormant for the rest of winter.

Tips

Use Mexican petunia on slopes, retaining walls or in large swaths as a groundcover for erosion control. It thrives in low-maintenance areas. It is also excellent for tucking in between larger perennials in mixed beds, as ana edging for beds and walkways or in containers.

Recommended

R. brittoniana is evergreen to semi-evergreen. It has dark green, lance-shaped leaves. Its large, tubular flowers in shades of purple, pink or white bloom early summer through frost. The dwarf varieties 'Katie' and **Bonita**™ have proven to stay compact and non-invasive. 'Katie' produces purple flowers, and Bonita™ produces light pink flowers.

Features: evergreen to semi-evergreen; purple, pink or white flowers; fast growing **Height:** 6–8"
Spread: 24" **Hardiness:** zones 8–11

Mexican petunia is disease and insect resistant. It is a Texas Superstar® plant.

Perennial Salvia
Salvia

S. greggii 'Furman's Red' (above), *S. farinacea* 'Victoria' (below)

Perennial salvias are reliable, hardy plants and a must-have in low-maintenance Texas gardens.

Growing

Perennial salvias prefer **full sun** but tolerate some shade. The soil should be of **average fertility, humus rich** and **well drained**. The plants are drought tolerant once established.

Deadhead to prolong blooming. Trim plants back in spring to encourage new growth and to keep them tidy. New shoots can sprout from old, woody growth; however, if you leave some salvias un-pruned for too long, they become sparse in the center.

Salvias are a favorite of bees.

Tips

Perennial salvias are attractive plants for a mixed perennial bed or container. Use them in low-maintenance medians and easements where irrigation may not be available.

Recommended

S. farinacea (mealy cup sage, blue sage) has bright blue flowers clustered along stems powdered with silver. **'Henry Deulberg'** is a vigorous spreader with pale blue flowers, and **'Indigo Spires'** produces masses of true blue flowers. Both are Texas Superstar® plants. **'Victoria Blue'** is a compact favorite.

S. greggii (autumn sage) is a dwarf, evergreen shrub that is often grown as a perennial. It grows 12–24" tall and wide and produces softly hairy foliage with snapdragon-like, red, purple, pink or yellow flowers from late summer to fall. Cultivars are available with bright reddish flowers. (Zones 7–9)

S. guaranitica (anise sage) has electric blue, tubular flowers from midsummer through fall. **'Black and Blue'** is one of the more striking varieties, with dark calyces and deep blue flowers.

S. leucantha (Mexican bush sage) is a Texas Superstar® plant with silver foliage and tall spikes of lavender blooms in fall. **'Santa Barbara'** is an excellent dwarf variety, growing only to 24" tall.

Also called: sage **Features:** cream, purple, blue or pink flowers; foliage **Height:** 12"–5' **Spread:** 12–24" **Hardiness:** zones 5–9

Pincushion Flower

Scabiosa

S. columbaria 'Butterfly Blue'

There are not many perennials that work as hard as this one in the Texas garden. Plants are almost non-stop bloomers all year long, taking a break only during the coldest weather.

Growing

Pincushion flowers grow best in **full sun**. The soil should be of **average to rich fertility, alkaline, well drained** and **rich in organic matter**. Keep the soil moderately moist, but do not overwater. The plants are drought tolerant once established.

While it's not required, regular deadheading will result in ever more flowers.

Tips

Pincushion flowers are perfect for the front of mixed perennial beds, rock gardens and retaining walls. They also do well in containers. Their continuous blooms make them a great cut-flower resource.

Recommended

S. columbaria is a compact, mounding perennial with soft gray-green leaves that blooms almost year-round in mild climates. **'Butterfly Blue,' 'Giant Blue'** and **'Pink Mist'** are all excellent cultivars.

The rounded, densely petaled blooms serve as a perfect landing pad for butterflies and bees.

Features: unique purple, blue, maroon, pink, white, red or bronze flowers; form; habit **Height:** 12–24" **Spread:** 12–36" **Hardiness:** zones 3–8

Shasta Daisy
Leucanthemum

Shasta daisy is one of the most popular perennials because it is easy to grow and the blooms are bright and plentiful.

Growing
Shasta daisy grows well in **full sun** or **partial shade**. Plants often thrive in morning sun with afternoon shade. The soil should be **fertile, moist** and **well drained**.

Pinch or trim plants back in spring to encourage compact, bushy growth. Deadheading extends the bloom by several weeks.

Start seeds indoors in spring or direct sow into warm soil. Divide every year or two in spring to maintain plant vigor.

Tips
Use shasta daisy as a single plant or massed in groups. Shorter varieties can be used in many garden settings; taller forms may need support if exposed to windy situations.

Recommended
L. × superbum forms a large clump of dark green leaves and stems. It bears white flowers with yellow centers all summer, often until first frost. **'Alaska'** bears large flowers and is hardier than the species. **'Becky'** has strong, wind-resistant stems and blooms lasting up to eight weeks.

The flowers can be cut for fresh arrangements.

L. × superbum (above & below)

Features: early summer to fall, white flowers with yellow centers **Height:** 12"–4' **Spread:** 15–24" **Hardiness:** zones 4–9

Stonecrop
Sedum

S. *acre* (above), S. 'Autumn Joy' (below)

Many stonecrop selections are grown for their foliage, which can range in color from steel gray-blue and green to red and burgundy.

Growing

Stonecrops prefer **full sun** but tolerate partial shade. The soil should be of **average fertility, very well drained** and **neutral to alkaline**.

Early summer pruning of upright species and hybrids encourages compact, bushy growth but can delay flowering. Divide in spring when needed.

Some 300 to 500 species of Sedum *are distributed throughout the Northern Hemisphere.*

Features: summer to fall flowers; decorative, fleshy foliage **Height:** 2–24" **Spread:** 12–24" or more **Hardiness:** zones 3–8

Tips

Low-growing stonecrops make wonderful groundcovers and additions to low-water or xeriscape gardens, retaining walls beds, mixed perennial beds or easements. They also edge beds and borders beautifully. Taller stonecrops give a lovely late-season display in a bed or border.

Recommended

There are many species, hybrids, cultivars and varieties to choose from, ranging from groundcover selections to tall, upright plants. They bloom at different times, but some of the more popular stonecrops are known for their fall blooms. Consult your local garden center for recommendations based on your gardening requirements.

Thrift

Phlox

P. subulata (above), 'Candy Stripe' (below)

A profuse bloomer for two to four weeks early in the year, this prostrate, creeping perennial always offers up a cheerful welcome in spring.

Growing

Plant thrift in **full sun** for the best blooms; late afternoon shade is tolerated. Plants are adapted to many different soil conditions, but **well-drained** soil is best. Thrift tolerates heat and drought.

Thrift attracts butterflies.

Shear flowers off after plants finish blooming to encourage lush new foliage growth. Fertilize after the bloom period is finished.

Tips

Use this evergreen bloomer as an edging for perennial beds, retaining walls, rock gardens and pathways. Tuck it into spaces around roses and perennials that may be dormant in late winter or early spring. Thrift is also excellent in containers.

Recommended

P. subulata is a small, creeping, evergreen perennial that is herbaceous when young but can become semi-woody over time. It is one of the earliest perennials to bloom in spring, when it is covered with pink, blue, lavender or white flowers. It has small, needle-like leaves. Out of bloom, it resembles a large patch of moss. Cultivars are available.

Features: evergreen foliage; pale blue, lavender, pink or white, early spring flowers **Height:** 6" **Spread:** 36" **Hardiness:** zones 3–9

Turk's Cap
Malvaviscus

A most versatile Texas native, this shrubby perennial sports unique whorled flowers that provide nectar to hummingbirds and certain species of butterflies.

Growing

Turk's cap can be grown in **full sun to full shade**. Plants in **full sun** locations can sometimes develop fungal issues on the leaves, but tend to bloom heavier. Turk's cap tolerates many soil conditions. Plants that establish in heavy, clay soils can be difficult to transplant. It is drought tolerant once established.

In southern parts of Texas, plants are evergreen; plants in northern parts of the state typically drop their leaves in winter. Plants are root hardy in most of the state. After the first hard freeze, Turk's cap can be cut down to the ground.

Tips

Use Turk's cap in shaded locations where you need to fill in large areas, as it will quickly grow and spread.

Recommended

M. drummondii forms a large, upright clump with tall stems and mallow-like, light green leaves. It usually blooms summer through fall; however, it can bloom year-round in warmer parts of the state. There are newer cultivars available. **'Fiesta'** has variegated foliage with yellow and white splotched leaves and is a Texas Superstar® plant. **'Pam Puryear'** sports soft pink flowers.

'Pam Puryear'

Turk's cap is naturally found growing in a variety of different habitats, from sandy streambeds to heavy clay soils in wooded areas.

Features: mallow-like foliage; bright red or white, whorled flowers; small berries; fast growing **Height:** 3–6'; up to 9' **Spread:** 3–5' **Hardiness:** zones 7–11

Yarrow
Achillea

A. millefolium 'Paprika' (above), *A. filipendulina* (below)

Yarrows make excellent groundcovers. They send up shoots and flowers from a low basal point and may be mowed periodically without excessive damage to the plant. Mower blades should be kept at least 4" high.

Yarrows are informal, tough plants with a fantastic color range. Their fine foliage provides texture interest in the garden and the flowers are irresistible to butterflies.

Growing

Grow yarrows in **full sun** in **well-drained** soil of **average fertility**—amend soils with compost if you have heavy clay. Yarrows tolerate drought and poor soil and abide, but do not thrive in, heavy, wet soil or very humid conditions. Excessively rich soil or too much nitrogen results in weak, floppy growth.

Deadhead to prolong blooming. Once the flowerheads begin to fade, cut them back to the lateral buds. Basal foliage should be left in place over the winter and tidied up in spring. Divide every two or three years in spring to maintain plant vigor.

Tips

Cottage gardens, wildflower gardens and mixed borders are the perfect places for these informal plants. Yarrows thrive in hot, dry locations where nothing else will grow.

Recommended

Many yarrow species, cultivars and hybrids are available.

A. filipendulina forms a clump of ferny foliage and bears yellow flowers. It has been used to develop several hybrids and cultivars.

A. millefolium (common yarrow) forms a clump of soft, finely divided foliage and bears white flowers. Many cultivars exist in a wide range of flower colors.

Features: white, yellow, red, orange, pink or purple, midsummer to early fall flowers; attractive foliage; spreading habit **Height:** 6"–4' **Spread:** 12–36" **Hardiness:** zones 3–9

Agave
Agave

Like yuccas, these architectural succulents are botanical relatives of lilies and are often referred to as "woody lilies." They make bold focal points in landscapes and containers.

Growing

Most agaves need **full sun** to thrive, but a bit of afternoon shade is tolerated. They perform best in **well-drained** soil. Agaves may need winter protection in the colder parts of the state.

Once established, agaves are very heat and drought tolerant. But to keep them thriving, water once a week in the heat of summer, less often in spring and fall and only minimally in winter; winter rainfall typically suffices.

A. americana (above), A. americana 'Marginata' (below)

Most agaves grow quite large and can be armed with dangerous spines at the ends and edges of their leaves. You can clip the ends of spines with sharp pruners. Small "pups" can be divided from the mother plant and transplanted.

Tips

Use agaves as striking focal points in landscape beds, low-maintenance easements and large containers. Combine them with low-water shrubs, perennials and grasses. Because of the spines, it's best to place them out of the way of pathways or areas frequented by children.

Features: summer blooms; large, pointed or rounded leaves in a rosette; many foliage colors; drought tolerant and easy to grow **Height:** 1–15' **Spread:** 1–20' **Hardiness:** zones 7–9

Recommended

These succulents come in many sizes and colors, with foliage in rosettes. Some species stay very small, while others can reach up to 20' in diameter. **A. americana**, a Texas native, is one of the largest and most beautiful. It can grow up to 6' tall, with gray-blue and silver foliage. Several varieties are available.

Other species good for landscape use include **A. bracteosa, A. filifera, A. harvardiana, A. lechuguilla, A. lophantha, A. neomexicana, A. ochahui, A. parryi, A. salmiana, A. scabra, A. schidigera, A. striata, A. victoria-reginae** and **A. weberi.**

Most species of agave are native to Mexico, with several also native to Texas.

Bald-Cypress
Taxodium

T. distichum (above & below)

Bald-cypress is a tough, dependable tree that can grow well in a variety of conditions and climates.

Growing

Bald-cypress grows well in **full sun**, in **acidic, moist** soil, but it can adapt to most soils and conditions. Highly alkaline soil may cause the foliage to turn yellow (chlorotic), although a particular strain from the Frio River in west Texas performs brilliantly in very alkaline soil.

Bald-cypress develops a deep taproot but transplants fairly easily when young.

Tips

Bald-cypress can be used as a specimen tree or in a group planting. This fairly large tree looks best with plenty of space around it—it is ideal in a swampy or frequently wet area where few other trees would thrive.

When grown in waterlogged soil or near a water feature, bald-cypress develops gnome-like "knees," which are knobby roots that poke up from the water.

Recommended

T. distichum is a slender, conical tree that may grow over 100' tall in the wild. With maturity, it becomes irregular and more rounded, and the trunk becomes buttressed. In fall, the blue-green foliage turns a rusty orange before falling.

People unfamiliar with bald-cypress usually expect it to be evergreen. Gasps are often heard when this deciduous conifer turns color in fall and defoliates. Plant near water to double the effect of its fall color.

Features: conical, coniferous, deciduous tree; attractive habit, trunk and foliage; cones; fall color **Height:** 50–70' or more **Spread:** 18–30' **Hardiness:** zones 4–9

Boxwood

Buxus

Boxwoods define formality in gardens. These versatile evergreens can be pruned to form neat hedges, geometric shapes or fanciful creatures.

Growing

Boxwoods prefer **partial shade** but adapt to full shade or to full sun if kept well watered. The soil should be **fertile** and **well drained**. Once established, boxwoods are drought tolerant.

It is best not to disturb the earth around established boxwoods. Refrain from using leaf blowers around boxwoods if possible. Mulch benefits these shallow-rooted shrubs.

Tips

These shrubs make excellent background plants in mixed borders. While they are most commonly continually sheared as boxed hedges, when allowed to grow naturally, they form attractive, rounded mounds.

Recommended

B. microphylla var. *koreana* (Korean littleleaf boxwood) is pest resistant and more tolerant of heat and humidity than common boxwood. It grows about 4' tall, with an equal spread. The bright green foliage may turn bronze, brown or yellow in winter. A number of cultivars are available.

'Green Mountain' (above), *B. microphylla* (below)

B. sempervirens (common boxwood) can grow up to 20' tall, with an equal spread, if it is not pruned. Cultivars are available in varied sizes and forms. **'Suffruticosa'** (edging boxwood) is a compact, slow-growing cultivar that is often used as hedging.

Some of the best boxwood selections are cultivars developed from crosses between the two listed species. These hybrids possess attractive winter color, vigor and a high level of pest resistance. **'Green Velvet'** and **'Green Mountain'** are good selections. **'Green Tower'** is a narrow, upright specimen.

Boxwood foliage contains toxic compounds that, when ingested, can cause severe digestive upset and possibly death.

Features: dense, rounded, evergreen shrub; bright green foliage; slow, even growth **Height:** 4–20'
Spread: equal to or slightly greater than height
Hardiness: zones 4–8

Chaste Tree
Vitex

V. agnus-castus (above & below)

Chaste tree's abundant, long-lasting, purple flowers make quite an impression, especially when this shrub has reached maturity. There is nothing more stunning in early summer than a chaste tree in bloom.

Growing
Chaste tree prefers **full sun** but tolerates partial shade. Any **well-drained, loamy** soil will do.

Chaste trees often grow much wider than is expected, so be sure to give yours plenty of room to grow to its mature size; don't plant it too close to your driveway. Shearing an established chaste tree that has outgrown its space typically ruins the overall form.

Chaste tree does not have an extensive root system, so when transplanting, be sure you don't damage the few roots it possesses. The roots should not be exposed to sun or wind while transplanting, which should be done in spring.

Tips
This shrub is often integrated into large mixed shrub and perennial borders, but it is equally if not more effective when planted as a specimen. Even when not in flower, chaste tree's ornate, scented foliage is striking. If possible, plant this shrub near sunny patios and windows so you can enjoy the fragrance.

Recommended
V. agnus-castus is an open, deciduous shrub with a spreading habit. It bears leaves that emerge from a central stem, similar in appearance to a hand with outstretched fingers. The aromatic foliage is complimented by fragrant, purple flowers borne in upright panicles in early to midsummer. The flower panicles themselves can grow 12–18" in length. Cultivars are available.

Chaste tree will attract butterflies to your garden.

Features: deciduous tree or shrub; open, rounded habit; aromatic, ornate foliage; purple to blue flowers **Height:** 10–15' **Spread:** 10–15' **Hardiness:** zones 6–9

Chinese Arborvitae

Platycladus

Arborvitaes offer evergreen structure and texture to the landscape. They are often used as large screening shrubs and hedges. Their soft needles are easy on the eyes and the hands.

Growing

Arborvitaes prefer **full sun** but will tolerate afternoon shade. The soil should be of **average fertility, alkaline, moist** and **well drained**. Arborvitaes enjoy humidity and are often found growing near marshy areas. They are known for tolerating dusty conditions and high levels of air pollution.

To maintain their size and form, shearing is not recommended, but rather selective hand pruning.

Tips

Large varieties of arborvitae make excellent specimen trees. Smaller cultivars can be used in foundation plantings and shrub borders, and as formal or informal hedges.

Recommended

P. orientalis (*Thuja orientalis*) is a narrow, pyramidal tree with scale-like needles. Two popular selections are **'Degroot's Spire,'** a slow-growing variety with deep green foliage and a mature size of 6' tall and 2' wide; and **'Golden Globe,'** a rounded, dwarf form with golden yellow foliage.

'Degroot's Spire'

Features: small to large, evergreen shrub or tree; blue-green foliage; bark; form **Height:** 15–25' **Spread:** 10–15' **Hardiness:** zones 2–9

Chinese arborvitae is available in several forms, including dwarf selections and those with brightly colored foliage.

Chinese Fringe-Flower
Loropetalum

L. chinense (above & below)

In the coldest parts of the state, Zone 6, if the plant is frozen to the ground in winter, it will regrow from the roots in spring.

Chinese fringe-flower is an attractive, spring-flowering shrub that can be used almost anywhere a large shrub is desired. The varieties with reddish purple leaves are a knockout.

Growing
Chinese fringe-flower grows best in **full sun** but does almost as well in partial or light shade. The ideal soil is **acidic, moist** and **well drained**, with a lot of **organic matter** mixed in, but Chinese fringe-flower adapts to sandy or clay soils. Once established, plants are drought tolerant; however, they require regular watering when newly planted.

Plants are best left to grow in their natural form; shearing is not recommended. Perform selective hand-pruning to keep plants in bounds or to a desired size.

Tips
Chinese fringe-flower can be used in a wide variety of shrub and mixed beds and borders. The evergreen foliage makes a nice background for other flowering plants. The purple-leafed varieties are the most popular and are used to provide foliage contrast in both formal and informal landscapes.

Recommended
L. chinense is a fast-growing, irregular, rounded to upright, evergreen shrub with glossy, dark green foliage and fragrant, creamy white flowers. A number of excellent selections have reddish purple leaves and showy pink flowers. **'Plum Delight'** and **'Purple Pixie'** are excellent performers with a more compact size.

Also called: Chinese witch-hazel **Features:** low-growing, spreading, evergreen shrub; white or pink, spring flowers; attractive foliage color; low maintenance **Height:** 3–10' (up to 20' for the species) **Spread:** 4–6' **Hardiness:** zones 7–10

Chinese Pistache

Pistacia

P. chinensis (above & below)

This tree is the favorite of many gardeners because of its speedy growth, fall color and uses in the landscape. It is an excellent small shade tree for urban landscapes.

Growing

Grow Chinese pistache in **full sun** in **moderately fertile, very well-drained** soil. This tree can tolerate a wide variety of conditions, including drought, pollution, restricted root space and alkaline soil.

Chinese pistache does not respond well to pruning. Train to form when it is young. After that, prune minimally, if needed, in late winter.

Regular shallow watering may induce Verticillium wilt; occasional deep waterings are best.

Features: deciduous tree; foliage; flowers; fruit; erect to spreading habit **Height:** 30–60'
Spread: 30–60' **Hardiness:** zones 7–10

Tips

Chinese pistache can be used as a street or shade tree. It is effective planted beside a patio and does reasonably well in lawns.

Male flowers and female flowers are borne on separate plants. For fruit production, both male and female trees are necessary.

Recommended

P. chinensis has leathery, glossy, dark green foliage that turns a vivid orange to red in fall. The fragrant, inconspicuous flowers bloom in mid- to late spring. Spherical, red fruit follows the flowers on female trees. It is a Texas Superstar® plant.

Cleyera
Ternstroemia

T. gymnanthera (above), *T. gymnanthera* cultivar (below)

If you're looking for lush, evergreen foliage for your shady foundation beds or landscape areas, cleyera is sure to fit the bill.

Growing

Plant in **light shade** or **full shade** locations, or areas that only receive limited direct sun in the morning. Cleyera will not tolerate full sun locations. While cleyera tends to prefer a slightly **acidic** soil, it is tolerant of a variety of soil conditions.

Cleyera is easy to maintain once established, but provide regular water to a young plant and then regularly through summer once established. It may need winter protection in the colder parts of the state.

Cleyera does not respond well to shearing or hedging; tip prune with hand pruners to keep it in bounds or to reduce the size.

Tips

Use cleyera as an evergreen foundation planting for northern or eastern exposures, as natural-form hedges or as background shrubs in shady beds.

Recommended

T. gymnanthera sports glossy, deep green leaves; new foliage emerges with orange to bronze coloring. Small, white flowers are produced in spring on the previous year's growth and are followed by small, oval berries in fall. **Le Ann**™ is a cultivar that produces bright red berries in fall. **Bronze Beauty**™ is a cultivar that is slightly more compact than other types. Its foliage emerges an attractive bronze color.

The dense foliage of cleyera makes it useful as an urban sound barrier.

Features: evergreen shrub; shade tolerant; dark, glossy foliage; white, spring flowers; fall fruit **Height:** 8–12' **Spread:** 5–8' **Hardiness:** zones 7–10

Crapemyrtle
Lagerstroemia

Crapemyrtle is a classic shrub and small tree in landscapes across Texas. Its long blooming season and ease of care makes it a popular choice for home gardens and municipal plantings.

Growing

Crapemyrtle performs best in a **full sun** location. It likes **neutral to slightly acidic, well-drained** soil. Water regularly to start. It is drought tolerant once established, but does best with occasional deep watering to encourage good blooming. Do not water from overhead.

Remove dead wood and old seed pods in spring. Shearing plants back (referred to as "crape murder") will not encourage more blooms; it will, however, ruin the beautiful natural form of the shrub as well as cause large knots at the point of hard pruning.

This tree may produce suckers and readily self-seeds. Once planted, it does not like to be moved.

Tips

There is a big size range in crapemyrtle varieties; be sure to select the right variety for your intended space.

Recommended

L. indica bears showy clusters of ruffled, crepe-like flowers in white, red, pink or purple all summer. The bronze-tinged, light green foliage ages to glossy, dark green in summer and turns yellow, orange or red in fall. The gray-brown bark exfoliates to reveal the pinkish bark beneath.

L. indica (above & below)

Many cultivars are available in a range of sizes and colors. **'Arapaho'** and **'Dynamite'** are popular red cultivars; **'Baton Rouge'** and **'Dallas Red'** are popular pinks; **'Catawba'** is an excellent purple; **'Acoma'** and **'Natchez'** are stellar whites. There are also new cultivars on the market that offer purple foliage, such as the **Black Diamond™ Series,** **'Delta Jazz'** and **First Editions® Series**.

In very alkaline or salty soil, crapemyrtle may show burnt leaf margins or chlorosis or both.

Features: upright, deciduous tree or shrub; white, pink, red or purple flowers; attractive foliage with excellent fall color; smooth, exfoliating bark **Height:** 2–25' **Spread:** 2–25' **Hardiness:** zones 7–10

Desert Willow

Chilopsis

C. *linearis* (above & below)

One of Texas' best native trees for ornamental use, these drought-tolerant beauties will steal the show in any urban garden or natural landscape setting.

Growing

A **full sun** location and **well-drained** soil are musts for desert willow. Do not plant in areas with excess or regular irrigation. In regions that receive more than 30" of rainfall, amend soil and raise the grade to provide better drainage. During its first year, water weekly, then reduce water as desert willow establishes.

Desert willow blooms on new wood, so regular selective hand pruning to remove spent growth will encourage more flowers.

Tips

Their compact size makes desert willows excellent candidates for small gardens and urban landscapes. Plants can be left to grow as multi-trunked shrubs or pruned into a tree form. Desert willows are deciduous but offer an interesting architectural form in the winter months.

Recommended

C. linearis is a relative of trumpet vine and esperanza. This small, deciduous Texas native blooms heavily summer through fall. There are a number of varieties and cultivars available. **'Bubba,' 'Dark Storm'** and **'White Storm'** are popular, excellent performers.

Desert willows attract hummingbirds, butterflies and moths.

Features: deciduous tree; willow-shaped foliage; white, pink, rose, violet or lavender, trumpet-shaped, fragrant blooms summer through fall; long, narrow seed pods **Height:** 15–20' **Spread:** 15–20' **Hardiness:** zones 7–10

Dwarf Palmetto
Sabal

S. minor

If you want to combine the look of a tropical garden with the low-maintenance nature of a Texas native, then dwarf palmetto is the right choice. This tough Texas palm makes an excellent evergreen shrub.

Growing

Although it can be planted in full sun, dwarf palmetto thrives in **light shade** as an understory shrub. Dwarf palmetto prefers **moist** soil; it is found growing naturally in areas of higher moisture, but it can adapt to drier conditions and a variety of soils once established. Water regularly until it is established, and provide supplemental water in summer months.

Dwarf palmetto is easily propagated from fresh seeds. Remove spent foliage at the base of the stem to keep it looking tidy.

Features: slow-, low-growing, evergreen shrub; bluish green, fan-shaped foliage; small, white, spring flowers; small, black, edible fruit **Height:** 5–6' **Spread:** 5–6' **Hardiness:** zones 6b–10

Tips

Dwarf palmettos are good for planting along streams or in landscaped areas that may stay wet or collect drainage from irrigation. They can also be established in large containers.

Recommended

S. minor is an evergreen, low-growing palm native to areas of Texas, Oklahoma, Arkansas and North Carolina. It is compact and without a visible main trunk, as it remains underground.

S. mexicana (Texas palmetto, Mexican palmetto) is a larger specimen that can develop a visible trunk above ground after many years and reach 30–40' tall. Texas palmetto and dwarf palmetto are often identified incorrectly as the same plant.

The edible fruits have a flavor similar to dates.

Elaeagnus
Elaeagnus

E. pungens 'Maculata' (above & below)

Elaeagnus is a tough-as-nails shrub that withstands drought, heavy soils, salty conditions and pollution. The evergreen foliage makes it a perfect low-maintenance privacy screening plant.

Use elaeagnus for contrast in large shrub beds. Full sun and dry conditions bring out the best silver color in the foliage.

Growing
Grow elaeagnus in **full sun** or **partial shade**. It prefers a **well-drained, sandy loam** of **average to high fertility** but can adapt to poor, heavy clay soil. Elaeagnus requires little if any watering after the second or third year in the ground. Young plants will need supplemental water during times of high heat and drought.

Although elaeagnus tolerates shearing and hedging, it looks much more attractive when tip pruned to accent its natural shape.

Tips
This tough plant works well in shrub or mixed borders and in hedges or screens. It is also useful for erosion control and soil stabilization. A tolerance for pollution and salty, dry conditions makes it useful for plantings along highways.

Recommended
E. pungens (thorny elaeagnus) is a spiny, evergreen shrub that spreads by suckers. The foliage is dark silvery green on top and silvery white beneath. Fragrant, tiny, silvery white flowers are produced in fall. The subsequent fruit, which begins brown and ripens to red, attracts wildlife, but the shrub is resistant to deer and rabbits. **'Variegata'** has yellow leaf margins.

Also called: silverthorn **Features:** large, sprawling, evergreen shrub; arching canes; fragrant flowers; summer foliage; easy to grow **Height:** 10–15' **Spread:** 10–15' **Hardiness:** zones 7–10

Elm
Ulmus

While Dutch elm disease has destroyed many of the American elms around the country, there are several other elms that are excellent for Texas landscapes.

Growing

Elm grows well in **full sun** or **partial shade**. It prefers a **moist, fertile, well-drained** soil but adapts to most soil types and conditions. It tolerates urban conditions, including pollution.

Elms are prolific seeders, so be prepared to deal with elm seedlings that will come up in your garden each year. Otherwise, elms are low maintenance.

Tips

Often a large tree, elm is attractive where it has plenty of room to grow, such as on large properties and in parks. Small cultivars make attractive specimen and shade trees.

Recommended

There are several elm species and cultivars available, with varied sizes, shapes and appeal, but the following are some of the highly recommended selections based on ease of growth and resistance to disease.

U. alata (winged elm) is a native, medium-sized tree that grows 30–40' tall with a rounded canopy with "winged" stems.

U. crassifolia (cedar elm) is a wide-spreading, open tree that grows up to 60' tall. It is a tough shade tree with beautiful golden fall color and is the most common native elm in Texas.

U. parviflora (above), *U. americana* (below)

U. parviflora (Chinese elm, lacebark elm) has a variable growth habit ranging from rounded to upright and vase-like, and it grows 40–50' tall and wide. 'Drake' is a good cultivar.

Elm seeds are a tasty treat for many small birds. These trees also provide shelter and nesting sites, attracting not only birds but other small wildlife as well.

Features: deciduous tree; attractive, rounded to vase-shaped habit; fall color; attractive, mottled bark **Height:** 30–80' or more **Spread:** 30–60' **Hardiness:** zones 5–9

Flowering Quince
Chaenomeles

'Texas Scarlet' (above & below)

Beautiful in and out of flower, flowering quince creates an attractive display as a specimen or when trained to grow up or along a brick wall.

Growing
Flowering quince grows best in **full sun**; it tolerates partial shade but produces fewer flowers. The soil should be of **average fertility, moist, slightly acidic** and **well drained**. This shrub is tolerant of pollution and urban conditions.

This shrub blooms on old wood, so prune only after it has finished blooming in spring.

Tips
Flowering quince can be included in shrub and mixed borders. It is very attractive when grown against a wall, and its spiny habit makes it useful for barriers. Use it along the edge of a woodland or in a naturalistic garden. The dark stems stand out in winter.

One of the loveliest of the late winter shrubs, quince adds drama and color on even the coldest days.

Recommended
C. speciosa (common flowering quince) is a large, tangled, spreading shrub. It grows 6–10' tall and spreads 6–15'. Red, white, pink or coral flowers are borne in late winter, followed by fragrant, greenish yellow fruit. Many cultivars are available, including the popular **'Toyo-Nishiki,'** which produces red, pink and white flowers all on the same plant. **'Cameo'** is a low, compact selection with double, apricot pink blooms. **'Jet Trail'** is also a low grower but has pure white blossoms. **'Texas Scarlet'** produces bright red flowers and is also known for its fruit.

Features: spreading, deciduous shrub; spiny branches; red, pink, white or orange, spring flowers; fragrant fruit **Height:** 2–10' **Spread:** 2–15' **Hardiness:** zones 5–8

Fringe Tree
Chionanthus

$\mathcal{F}$ringe tree is a beautiful shrub that is native to the eastern parts of the state. It is adaptable to a wide range of growing conditions. Early summer sees it densely covered in silky, honey-scented flowers that shimmer in the breeze.

Growing

Fringe tree prefers **full sun**. It does best in soil that is **fertile, acidic, moist** and **well drained** but adapts to most soil conditions.

This plant achieves an attractive multi-stemmed, mounding form if left unpruned. However, you can remove the lower branches on a young plant to train it into a more classic tree form.

C. virginicus (above & below)

Tips

Fringe tree works well as a specimen plant, as part of a border or beside a water feature. It flowers at a very early age. The fruit attracts birds.

Recommended

C. virginicus (white fringe tree) is a spreading, small tree or large shrub that bears fragrant, drooping, white flowers. Both male and female flowers are needed for fruit to form. They are usually borne on separate plants, but sometimes both sexes appear on the same plant.

Fringe tree can be difficult to find in general nurseries, but it is becoming more available every year. Specialty nurseries and plant sales at botanical gardens, universities or colleges are likely places to find it.

Also called: grancy gray-beard **Features:** rounded or spreading, deciduous large shrub or small tree; white, early summer flowers; attractive bark and habit **Height:** 10–25' **Spread:** 10–25' **Hardiness:** zones 4–8

Ginkgo

Ginkgo

G. biloba (above & below)

There is not a leaf in the tree kingdom that is as distinctive and elegant as a ginkgo leaf. This tree is the perfect choice if you're looking for both architectural form and stunning fall color.

Growing

In Texas, ginkgo prefers **full sun** but appreciates some shade from larger trees in the late afternoon. The soil should be **fertile, sandy** and **well drained**, but this tree adapts to most conditions. It is also tolerant of urban environments.

If you buy an unnamed plant, be sure it has been propagated from cuttings. Seed-grown trees may prove to be female, and the stinky fruit is not something you want dropping on your lawn, driveway or sidewalk.

Tips

Although its growth is very slow, ginkgo eventually becomes a large tree that is best suited as a specimen tree in parks and large gardens. It can also be used as a street tree.

Recommended

G. biloba is variable in habit. The uniquely fan-shaped leaves can turn an attractive shade of yellow in fall. There are quite a few named varieties available, including variegated, weeping and dwarf selections. **'Autumn Gold'** grows 40' tall and offers up especially bold fall color; **'Pendula'** is a weeping dwarf selection good as a smaller specimen in landscape beds or containers; and **'Troll'** is a very compact specimen perfect for patio containers.

Ginkgo sheds nearly all of its golden fall leaves within a single day, making raking a snap.

Also called: maidenhair tree **Features:** deciduous tree; conical habit in youth, variable with age; summer and fall foliage; bark; pest free **Height:** 40–100'; dwarf varieties 2–12' **Spread:** 10–100' or more; dwarf varieties vary **Hardiness:** zones 3–9

Glossy Abelia
Abelia

Glossy abelia is blessed with attractive foliage, great flowers and interesting bark. This striking, easy-to-grow shrub can attract butterflies, praying mantises and hummingbirds to your garden.

Growing

Glossy abelia prefers **full sun** but tolerates partial afternoon shade. The soil should be **slightly acidic, fertile, moist** and **well drained**, although glossy abelia is adaptable to different soils and extremely drought tolerant once established.

In most areas of Texas, glossy abelia is evergreen; in the coldest parts of the state, it is semi-evergreen. If parts of the top-growth are damaged or killed by cold, they will re-grow from the crown.

Tips

Glossy abelia is good for both formal and informal gardens and hedges, and it is attractive individually or in groups. It can be used in shrub or mixed borders. Clematis vines weave beautifully through glossy abelia. Standard varieties make excellent background shrubs for mixed beds, while dwarf varieties are perfect for placing closer to front entrances or walkways.

Recommended

A. × grandiflora produces white or pale pink flowers sporadically all summer. The glossy, dark green foliage turns red or bronze in fall, persisting through winter in mild areas. In colder areas, the leaves drop, revealing the attractive exfoliating stems. These shrubs are large, growing up to 8' tall. Variegated

A. × grandiflora (above & below)

and compact cultivars are available. **'Edward Goucher'** is typically the most widely known and available dwarf abelia. **'Kaleidoscope,'** a relatively new dwarf cultivar, offers variegated foliage with excellent fall color on 3' tall plants. **'Sherwoodii'** produces much smaller, finer leaves on 4' tall plants. **'Twist of Lime'** offers chartreuse foliage with cream edges.

Deer seem to avoid abelias that have been in the ground for more than two or three years.

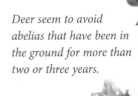

Features: large, rounded, evergreen or semi-evergreen shrub; white or pink flowers; attractive foliage and stems **Height:** 3–8' **Spread:** 4–8'
Hardiness: zones 6–9

Holly
Ilex

I. vomitoria (above), *I. cornuta* 'Nellie R. Stevens' (below)

Hollies are durable shrubs and trees that vary greatly in shape and size. When given conditions they like, they thrive for years.

Growing

These plants prefer **full sun** but tolerate partial shade. The soil should be of **average to high fertility, humus rich** and **moist**. Hollies perform best in **acidic** soil. Apply a summer mulch to keep the roots cool and moist. Fertilize bi-annually with a feed formulated for hollies and other acid-loving plants.

Holly hedges will require regular pruning, but specimen plants can simply be hand pruned as needed to keep their desired shape or size.

Although holly berries should be avoided by people, they are a reliable food source for birds and other wildlife.

Tips

Hollies can be used in groups, in woodland gardens and in shrub and mixed borders. Many types can also be shaped into hedges, topiary and espalier with hand pruners.

Recommended

The following holly species do very well in Texas gardens. Many cultivars of different sizes and leaf shapes are available for each of the species.

Evergreen shrub species include **I. crenata** (Japanese holly), **I. vomitoria** (yaupon), a Texas native, and **I. cornuta** (Chinese holly). **'Nellie R. Stevens,'** a hybrid of *I. cornuta* and *I. aquifolium*, is a vigorous, conical, evergreen shrub that can reach 20' tall and spread 10'. It produces the familiar spiny, glossy foliage and shiny, scarlet fruit.

Tree species include **I. opaca** (American holly), is a large, evergreen tree. **I. decidua** (possumhaw), another Texas native, is an upright, deciduous shrub with bright green foliage and red or orange fruit. **'Warren's Red'** is more upright and produces bright red fruit and lustrous foliage.

Features: deciduous or evergreen shrub or tree; decorative, glossy, often spiny foliage; fruit; attractive habit **Height:** 3–20' for shrub species; 40–50' for tree species **Spread:** 3–15' for shrub species; 30–40' for tree species **Hardiness:** zones 3–9

Juniper
Juniperus

Junipers are tough and versatile. A form, color and texture is available for most landscaping situations. There are many species native to Texas.

Growing

Junipers prefer **full sun** but tolerate light shade. The soil should be of **average fertility** and **well drained**, but these plants tolerate most conditions. Do not overwater.

Junipers do not need regular pruning and will not tolerate heavy pruning or regular shearing. They should only be pruned in a way that maintains their natural form.

Tips

Junipers make prickly barriers, hedges and windbreaks. They can be used in borders, as specimens or in groups. The low-growing species can be used in rock gardens and as groundcover. For interesting evergreen color, mix the yellow-foliaged junipers with blue-needled varieties.

Recommended

Junipers vary from species to species and often from cultivar to cultivar within a species. *J. chinensis* (Chinese juniper) is a conical tree or spreading shrub. *J. conferta* (shore juniper) is a bushy, prostrate shrub. *J. horizontalis* (creeping juniper) is a prostrate, creeping groundcover. *J. procumbens* (Japanese garden juniper) is a wide-spreading, low shrub.

The prickly foliage may give some gardeners a rash.

J. virginiana (above), *J. horizontalis* (below)

J. ashei (Texas cedar, ashe juniper, mountain cedar) is a Texas native that can be quite invasive, takes up large amounts of water and is also the source of common allergy problems across the state.

J. virginiana (eastern red-cedar) is a Texas native that has been widely used for its rot-resistant wood. While it has been more commonly planted as an ornamental specimen tree, the male trees also produce allergy-inducing pollen.

Features: conical or columnar tree, rounded or spreading shrub or prostrate groundcover; evergreen; variety of color, size and habit **Height:** 6"–70' **Spread:** 12"–25' **Hardiness:** zones 3–8

Mahonia
Mahonia

M. bealei (above & below)

Mahonia is a slow-growing, trouble-free shrub that is excellent for bringing interest to shady areas and attracting birds to your garden. When the blue, grape-like fruits are ripe, the birds devour them with gusto.

Growing

Mahonia prefers **light shade** or **partial shade**; it needs protection from the hot afternoon sun. The soil should be **neutral to slightly acidic, humus rich, moist** and **well drained**.

Only light, selective pruning is recommended; this shrub does not tolerate shearing.

Tips

Mahonia looks great in groups of three or more. Use it in mixed or shrub borders, as a specimen and in woodland gardens. It truly excels as a transition plant between a woodland garden and a more formal garden.

Recommended

M. bealei (leatherleaf mahonia) is an open, upright shrub. Its mildly fragrant, lemon yellow flowers are followed by clusters of light blue berries. The spiny-edged foliage is a dull blue-green and is very leathery.

M. eurybracteata 'Soft Caress' offers slender, bamboo-like foliage with bright yellow blooms and a compact habit; it grows 4' tall.

M. fortunei (Chinese mahonia) is an upright shrub with dark green, holly-like foliage and bright yellow flowers followed by round, dark blue berries with a hint of white. This species grows 4' tall and 3' wide.

M. repens (creeping mahonia) is a Texas native, low-growing, suckering shrub bearing sharply toothed foliage and dark yellow flowers, which are followed by blue-black berries. It grows to only 12" tall. Taller cultivars are available.

The juicy berries are edible but somewhat tart. They can be eaten fresh or used to make jellies, juices or wine—if you get to them before the birds do.

Features: open, upright, evergreen shrub; fragrant, yellow late-winter to spring flowers; late-spring to early-summer fruit; leathery foliage **Height:** 1–12' **Spread:** 3–10' **Hardiness:** zones 6–9

Maple
Acer

Maples are attractive year-round, with delicate flowers in spring, beautiful foliage and hanging samaras (winged fruit) in summer, vibrant leaf color in fall and interesting bark and branch structures in winter.

Growing

Generally, maples do well in **full sun** or **light shade**, though their light preferences vary by species. The soil should be **fertile, high in organic matter, moist** and **well drained**. Certain maples can tolerate wet soils, such as the red maple.

Tips

Use maples as specimen, shade or street trees, as large elements in shrub or mixed borders and as hedges.

Recommended

A. × freemanii **'Autumn Blaze'** is an improved hybrid good for urban landscapes.

A. grandidentatum (bigtooth maple) is a large native Texas specimen good for the Hill Country area.

A. rubrum (red maple) is a Texas native grown as a single- or multi-stemmed tree. It grows 40–60' tall, with a variable spread of 20–60'. The fall foliage color varies from bright yellow to orange or red. **'Drummond'** and **'October Glory'** are good cultivars.

A. truncatum (purpleblow maple, Shantung maple) is a compact, rounded tree with lush foliage that turns a bright yellow in fall.

Be sure to know the mature size of your chosen maple species so as not to interfere with power lines or other utilities.

A. rubrum (above), A. × freemanii cultivar (below)

Features: rounded, dense, deciduous tree or shrub; decorative foliage, bark and form; samaras; fall color; greenish flowers **Height:** 25–50' **Spread:** 25–40' **Hardiness:** zones 4–8

Mexican Plum
Prunus

P. mexicana

Mexican plum fruit can be eaten fresh or made into preserves. Birds and mammals also consume the fruit.

Nothing heralds the coming of spring like the highly fragrant, white blooms of the Mexican plum. With flowers, fruit and a compact size, Mexican plums are an all-in-one tree for small spaces or urban landscapes.

Growing
Plant Mexican plum in a **full sun** location or as an understory tree, as it will tolerate late-day shade. It typically prefers **well-drained** soil and it is naturally found growing in the rich soils of river bottoms, open wooded areas and prairie fields.

Plant it slightly above grade to ensure good drainage. This tree does not sucker, as many other native plums do.

Tips
Mexican plum is a spring-blooming specimen tree that is excellent for small spaces and urban settings because it rarely interferes with power lines.

Recommended
P. mexicana is a small, single-trunked tree with fragrant, white flowers before leaves emerge in spring. The attractive bark is dark and rough. This plum can grow anywhere from 15–35' tall but is most often seen in the 20–25' range. It is a Texas native.

Features: small, deciduous tree; fragrant, white, spring flowers; rosy pink, edible, summer fruit **Height:** 15–35' **Spread:** 15–35' **Hardiness:** zones 6-9

Nandina

Nandina

Nandina has so much to offer in the landscape, including glorious foliage and berry color, a tough constitution and an evergreen habit. Few other shrubs possess such year-round color and versatility.

Growing

Nandina prefers **full sun** but can also be grown in shadier conditions. It prefers a soil that is **humus rich, moist** and **well drained**; however, it thrives even in heavy clay. Nandina will grow faster if watered regularly, but established plants can tolerate extended periods of drought and neglect. Shrubs in full sun that experience some frost produce the best fall and winter color.

Do not shear; selectively hand prune to keep nandina to desired size.

Tips

Use nandina in shrub borders, as a background plant and for informal hedges or screens. The dwarf varieties are good in containers. Mass planting ensures a large quantity of the shiny, bright red berries.

The colorful berries of nandina persist through winter and attract birds, which then spread the seeds.

N. domestica (above & below)

Recommended

N. domestica produces clumps of thin, upright, lightly branched stems and fine, textured foliage. It grows 6–8' tall and spreads 3–5', slowly proliferating by suckering. It bears large, loose clusters of small, white flowers followed by persistent, spherical fruit. Initially tinged bronze to red, the foliage becomes light to medium green in summer, with many varieties turning red to reddish purple in fall and winter. Many cultivars are available, including '**Firepower**,' a dwarf selection with bright red foliage; '**Obsession**,' which offers a dwarf habit and colorful foliage; and '**Nana Purpurea**,' which produces fiery red winter foliage.

Also called: sacred bamboo, common nandina, heavenly bamboo **Features:** tough, long-lived, evergreen shrub; white, late spring to early summer flowers; fruit; decorative foliage **Height:** 18"–8' **Spread:** 18"–5' **Hardiness:** zones 6–9

Oak

Quercus

Q. macrocarpa (above), Q. virginiana (below)

The oak's classic shape, outstanding fall color, deep roots and long life are some of its many assets. While typically slow growing, this classic tree is most popularly used as a shade tree in our hot Texas climate.

Growing

Most oaks grow well in **full sun**, in **fertile, slightly acidic, moist, well-drained** soil. Oaks grow fast for their first 10 years of life and then slow down.

Oaks can be difficult to establish; transplant them only when they are young. Do not disturb the ground around the base of an oak; these trees are very sensitive to changes in grade.

Tips

Oaks are large trees that are best as specimens or for groves in parks and large gardens. Remember that live oaks are evergreen and will produce heavy shade year-round as they mature.

Recommended

Some of the best selections for Texas include *Q. buckleyi* (Texas red oak), a medium-sized Texas native with good fall color; *Q. macrocarpa* (bur oak, mossycup oak), a large, broad tree with furrowed bark that grows 50–80' tall and wide; *Q. polymorpha* (Mexican white oak, Monterrey oak), a medium-sized oak good for urban spaces that grows to 40' tall with rounded canopy; *Q. shumardii* (Shumard oak, Shumard red oak), a broad, spreading tree with red fall color that grows 40–70' tall and 40–60' wide; and *Q. virginiana* (live oak), a large evergreen native to Texas that is commonly used as a shade tree.

Oaks belong to one of two groups, the Red Oak Group (Erythrobalanus) or the White Oak Group (Lepidobalanus). Red oaks have leaves that are typically acutely lobed with hair-like awns on the edge and acorns that mature on the previous year's wood. White oaks have leaves that are typically round lobed with no awns and acorns that mature on the current season's wood.

Features: large, rounded, spreading, deciduous or evergreen tree; summer and fall foliage; attractive bark; acorns **Height:** 40–80' **Spread:** 40–100' **Hardiness:** zones 4–9

Oakleaf Hydrangea

Hydrangea

Oakleaf hydrangeas are one of the easiest and showiest shrubs to grow in a shade garden. The large blooms are impressive, and oak-shaped foliage often lights up with bright colors in fall.

Growing

Oakleaf hydrangeas grow best in **partial to full shade**. Direct morning sun is good, but plants do best with some protection from the hot afternoon sun. They prefer soil that is of **average to high fertility, humus rich, moist** and **well drained**, though you'll find oakleaf hydrangeas are tough in varied soil conditions once established. They tolerate dry conditions and do not like soggy conditions.

Hydrangeas produce blooms on the previous year's growth, so do not prune in spring; wait until plants have finished blooming to hand prune. They are semi-evergreen, so expect to lose some foliage in winter; however, the peeling bark that is revealed is attractive.

Tips

Oakleaf hydrangeas can be included in shrub or mixed shade beds, used as specimens or informal barriers, or planted in groups.

Recommended

H. quercifolia is a mound-forming, native shrub that spreads by suckers. It has attractive, exfoliating bark and large, oak-like leaves. Plants produce large, football-shaped clusters of white flowers. **'Alice'** can reach 15' tall and produces large, white blooms. **'Snowflake'** and **'Harmony'** offer double blooms. **'PeeWee'** is a dwarf variety that grows only 3–4' tall. **'Ruby Slippers'** offers pink blooms on dwarf, 4' tall plants.

H. quercifolia (above & below)

Traces of cyanide are found in the leaves and buds of some hydrangeas. Wash your hands well after handling these plants. Avoid burning the clippings because the smoke can be **toxic***.*

Features: mounding or spreading, deciduous shrub or small tree; showy, spring flowers; attractive habit, foliage and bark
Height: 3–15' **Spread:** 3–12' **Hardiness:** zones 3–8

Pomegranate
Punica

P. granatum (above & below)

This classic fruit tree makes for a stunning large landscape shrub across Texas. A tough constitution, showy blooms and beautiful, flavorful fruit make pomegranate a perfect fit for urban landscapes.

Growing
Pomegranate should be grown in **full sun**. It can grow in just about any type of soil, as long as it is **well drained**. Pomegranate is very heat and drought tolerant once established, but provide consistent moisture to new plants, or to plants you plan to harvest from heavily.

Pomegranate will sucker regularly, so keep suckers pruned away. Pruning of the main plant is rarely required, but do hand prune any deadwood out regularly.

Tips
Although pomegranate can be trained as a small tree, it is more commonly grown as a large shrub. Large varieties make excellent specimen or anchor shrubs or small trees. Dwarf selections can be mixed into landscape beds or grown in containers.

Recommended
P. granatum is a deciduous or semideciduous shrub or small tree with glossy, dark green leaves and large, colorful fruit. There are a number of named varieties of pomegranate, each with slight variations in size, fruit color and cold hardiness. Dwarf varieties grown strictly for ornamental use are also available.

If you're in southern Texas, be sure to look for "low-chill" varieties such as 'Ambrosia,' 'Granada' or 'Wonderful,' which is the most commonly available variety; however, 'Pecos,' 'Sal,' 'Salavatski' and 'Texas Red' are rated to have better flavor. 'Russian 18' is a bit more cold-hardy and adapted to many parts of the state.

For best performance, choose the sunniest, warmest part of your garden for your pomegranate.

Features: deciduous to semi-deciduous large shrub or small tree; glossy, dark green foliage; showy, orange-red, spring and summer flowers; yellow to bright red, 2–4" fruit **Height:** 8–15'; dwarf varieties 2–5' **Spread:** 8–15'; dwarf varieties 2–5' **Hardiness:** zones 7–10; can be grown in zone 6 with winter protection

Redbud

Cercis

This outstanding native plant is often the first welcomer of spring in many landscapes. The intense, deep magenta buds open to pink flowers that cover the long, thin branches in clouds of color. Redbud is one of Texas' best understory trees.

Growing

Redbud grows well in **partial shade** or **light shade**; it appreciates some protection from the hottest afternoon sun. The soil should be **fertile, deep, moist** and **well drained**. This plant has tender roots and does not like being transplanted.

Tips

Redbud can be used as a specimen tree, in a shrub or mixed border and in a woodland garden. A locally grown redbud will perform best in your garden.

Recommended

C. canadensis (eastern redbud) is a spreading, multi-stemmed tree that bears red, purple, pink or occasionally white flowers. The young foliage is bronze, fading to green over summer and turning bright yellow in fall. Many beautiful cultivars and varieties are available, including **var. texensis** (Texas redbud), which bears waxy but glossy, rich green leaves and dark wine red flowers. **'Forest Pansy'** is a stunning cultivar with deep purple foliage.

C. canadensis

Redbud is not as long lived as many other trees, so use its delicate beauty to supplement more permanent trees.

Features: spreading, dense, deciduous tree or shrub; red, purple, pink or white, spring flowers; seedpods; fall color
Height: 15–30' **Spread:** 12–30' **Hardiness:** zones 6–9

Red Yucca

Hesperaloe

H. parviflora

A Texas native, red yucca is extremely tough and tolerates a variety of soil conditions, drought, heat and cold.

Not to be confused with true yuccas, red yucca is a staple in many landscapes in Texas and the southwest. Its grass-like, spiky foliage and long spikes of pink, red, coral and yellow flowers are a welcome surprise in locations often too inhospitable for other ornamental plants.

Growing

Plant red yucca in **full sun** for best performance. A **well-drained** soil is preferred because this plant doesn't tolerate soggy soil. It can be used areas that do not receive supplemental irrigation and little maintenance.

Pruning is not needed, but the flower spikes can be removed when flowering is finished, and dead leaves can be removed as needed.

Tips

Red yucca looks great in natural settings with other native plants such as Texas sage and perennial salvias. Use red yucca in areas where you may not have many other blooming plants or only short-blooming perennials.

Recommended

H. parviflora is a stemless succulent that produces clumps of arching, grass-like foliage and tall spikes of flowers that bloom from May through October. Several color variations are available ranging from light red to coral to yellow. Look for new cultivar **Brakelights**®, which bears intense, deep red flowers.

Features: attractive, succulent, evergreen, strap-like foliage; small, edible flowers in range of colors produced on tall spikes
Height: 3–5' **Spread:** 2–4' **Hardiness:** zones 5–11

Smoke Tree
Cotinus

Smoke tree produces inconspicuous yellow flowers in early summer. When the flower stalks mature, long, feather-like hairs emerge and change to pink or purple, giving the illusion that the tree is enveloped in a cloud of smoke.

Growing

Smoke tree grows well in **full sun** or **partial shade**. It prefers soil of **average fertility** that is **moist** and **well drained**. Established plants adapt to dry, sandy soils. Smoke tree is very tolerant of alkaline, gravelly soil.

Smoke tree has a beautiful natural form. However, if left un-pruned, it can become leggy over time. Prune back leggy growth after smoke tree has finished blooming to encourage new growth.

Tips

Smoke tree can be used in shrub or mixed landscape beds, as a single specimen or in groups. It is a good choice for a rocky hillside planting.

Recommended

C. coggygria is a bushy, rounded shrub that develops large, puffy plumes of flowers that start out green and gradually turn a pinky gray. The green foliage turns red, orange and yellow in fall. Many cultivars are available. **'Pink Champagne'** produces pink-beige flowers, **'Royal Purple'** has purplish red flowers and dark purple foliage, and **'Velvet Cloak'** bears dark burgundy foliage that turns reddish purple in fall.

'Royal Purple' (above), *C. coggygria* (below)

Smoke tree is fast growing and often grows wider than taller. Be sure to leave adequate space when planting it around driveways or sidewalks.

Also called: smokebush **Features:** bushy, rounded, spreading, deciduous tree or shrub; early summer flowers; summer and fall foliage; easy to grow **Height:** 8–15' **Spread:** 8–15' **Hardiness:** zones 4–8

Southern Wax Myrtle
Myrica

M. cerifera (above & below)

Southern wax myrtle is a wonderful native shrub that can stand alone as a specimen or blend easily into a mixed border. If you're looking for a moderately sized evergreen anchor shrub, you've found it.

Growing

Southern wax myrtle grows well in **full sun** or **partial shade**. It adapts to most soil conditions, from poor, sandy soil to heavy clay soil.

Southern wax myrtle rarely needs pruning and should not be sheared or hedged.

Tips

This adaptable plant forms large colonies and can be used for mass plantings in underused areas. Single plants can be included in large landscape beds or used as individual specimens.

Recommended

M. cerifera is a rounded, evergreen shrub. It takes on an upright form, bearing lance-shaped, aromatic foliage and inconspicuous greenish yellow catkins, followed by grayish white fruit that remains on the branches throughout winter. This species grows 15' tall and wide. **Var. *pumila*** (dwarf southern wax myrtle) mimics the look of the standard species but grows only 5–6' tall and wide. It can be used as a natural, unsheared hedge.

These plants fix nitrogen in the soil, much like legumes do, which may explain the ability of southern wax myrtle to perform well in poor soils.

Also called: bayberry **Features:** aromatic, evergreen shrub; foliage; dense, suckering habit; persistent fruit **Height:** 5–15' **Spread:** 5–15' **Hardiness:** zones 6–9

Spirea
Spiraea

S. *japonica* (above), S. × *vanhouttei* (below)

Spireas are old-fashioned shrubs that became cutting-edge choices when dwarf, colorful types were introduced. Now that groundcover varieties are available, spireas are approching cutting-edge status again.

Growing

Spireas prefer **full sun** but do benefit from late afternoon shade. To help prevent foliage burn, provide protection from very hot sun. The soil should be **fertile, acidic, moist** and **well drained**.

Spireas are popular because they adapt to a variety of situations and require only minimal care once established. When needed, prune right after blooming has finished.

Tips

Use spireas in shrub or mixed borders, in rock gardens and as informal screens and hedges.

Recommended

Many species and cultivars are available, including the following selections. **S. *japonica*** (Japanese spirea) forms a clump of erect stems and bears pink or white flowers. **S. *nipponica*** is an upright, spreading shrub with arching branches, dark green foliage and cup-shaped, white flowers in midsummer. **'Snowmound'** is a vigorous, spreading cultivar with a prolific flowering habit. **S. *prunifolia*** (bridalwreath spirea) is a large, arching shrub with finely toothed leaves and copious amounts of double, white flowers in late spring. **S. × *vanhouttei*** (Vanhoutte spirea) is a dense, bushy shrub with arching branches that bears clusters of white flowers. Many new cultivars available, with varying foliage colors and sizes.

Spireas are a favorite for attracting butterflies to the garden.

Features: round, bushy, deciduous shrub; summer flowers; habit **Height:** 2–8'
Spread: 2–8' **Hardiness:** zones 3–9

Texas Mountain Laurel

Sophora

S. secundiflora

Have you tried to grow lilacs in Texas, but realized that it's a tough task to accomplish? Texas mountain laurel is an excellent substitute. This Texas native is a stunning spring bloomer with a fragrance to rival even lilacs.

Growing

Texas mountain laurel prefers **full sun**, though it can tolerate some late afternoon shade. It prefers **well-drained** and somewhat **rocky, limestone** soil. Texas mountain laurel is very drought tolerant once established; do not over water.

The seeds contain the highly poisonous alkaloid cytosine, a substance related to nicotine that is used as a narcotic and hallucinogen. If the seeds are swallowed whole, there may be little to no damage. However, if seed coating is broken or seeds are chewed, they are highly toxic to people, pets and aquatic life.

This plant is slow growing, so you'll need to have some patience for it to reach its desired size. Fertilize in spring and fall to speed up the growth rate.

Treat Texas mountain laurel as a large shrub or small tree. Pruning is rarely required, but if needed, selectively hand prune; never shear.

Tips

Texas mountain laurel makes an excellent evergreen anchor plant in large landscape beds, or a stunning specimen large shrub or small tree. Plant it near entryways, windows and patios so you can enjoy the intense, grape fragrance. It is excellent for use in low-water, low-maintenance landscapes.

Recommended

S. secundiflora is native from central Texas west to New Mexico and south to San Luis Potosi in Mexico. An evergreen, spring-blooming member of the pea family, its compound leaves are made up of small, rounded leaflets. Its green seed pods contain shiny, red seeds.

Features: evergreen large shrub or small tree; glossy foliage; large, grape-like clusters of fragrant, lavender to purple, spring flowers **Height:** 10–15' **Spread:** 10' **Hardiness:** 7–11

Texas Sage
Leucophyllum

This beautiful, easy-care shrub is a staple in gardens all across Texas. It bursts into bloom throughout the growing season, filling the landscape with color and food for bees and butterflies.

L. langmaniae 'Rio Bravo' (above & below)

Growing

Plant Texas sage in a **full sun** location; plants that receive shade get thin and leggy. It can thrive in a variety of soil conditions as long as the soil is **well drained**. Once established, it is extremely heat and drought tolerant; do not overwater. It can be planted in areas without irrigation or that receive little to no regular maintenance. Texas sage may require winter protection in the coldest parts of the state.

Texas sage can be sheared, but it performs best when left to grow into its natural round or oval shape. Regular shearing will deprive you of regular blooming.

Tips

Use Texas sage in low-maintenance landscapes to provide foliage contrast and bloom color. Native to northern Mexico through Texas and into New Mexico, this tough shrub can be grown successfully with little care.

Recommended

L. candidum '**Thunder Cloud**' offers up deep purple flowers.

L. frutescens has many varieties, and all are excellent performers in Texas. '**Silverado**,' '**Desperado**,' '**Heavenly Cloud**' and '**Green Cloud**' are especially favored.

L. langmaniae '**Rio Bravo**' is a prolific bloomer with a wider growth habit.

There are little to no disease or pest problems associated with Texas sage other than cotton root rot in soils that do not drain properly.

Features: semi-evergreen to evergreen shrub; silver foliage; flowers in white, pink and various shades of purple **Height:** 5–8' **Spread:** 4–6' **Hardiness:** zones 8–10

Viburnum

Viburnum

V. × *burkwoodii* (above), V. *rufidulum* (below)

*V*iburnum is a large genus of excellent garden plants. In Texas, they are most often used in shady locations to provide evergreen foliage and blooms.

Growing

Viburnums grow best in **partial shade** or **light shade**. Certain types will tolerate more direct sun. The soil should be of **average fertility, slightly acidic, moist** and **well drained**. While generally low maintenance, viburnums prefer consistent moisture; mulch to conserve moisture.

Allow viburnums to achieve a natural form. Hand prune to maintain size or shape after blooming has finished.

Tips

Viburnums look great in the shade of evergreen trees. They are a good choice for plantings near patios, decks and swimming pools.

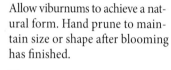

Recommended

Many viburnum species, hybrids and cultivars are available. Check with your local nursery for best options for your area.

V. × *burkwoodii* (Burkwood viburnum) is an upright to rounded, deciduous to semi-evergreen shrub. It grows 6–10' tall and spreads 5–8'. Clusters of fragrant, pinkish white flowers appear in mid- to late spring. The subsequent red fruit ripens to black. (Zones 4–8)

V. odoratissimum (sweet viburnum) is a medium- to fast-growing evergreen that produces clusters of white flowers in spring. It grows 12–15' tall and wide. (Zones 8–10)

V. rufidulum (rusty blackhaw viburnm) is a deciduous Texas native with glossy, green leaves, clusters of white flowers in spring and blue fruit in fall. It grows 10–30' tall. (Zones 5–9)

V. tinus 'Spring Bouquet' is a stellar performer in Texas. It is a dense, fast-growing evergreen that produces heavy clusters of white or pinkish blooms in spring and blue-black fruit in fall. It tolerates some direct sun and grows 6–10' tall and 4–6' wide. (Zones 7–11)

Features: evergreen or deciduous shrub; large foliage; fragrant, spring flowers **Height:** 6–30' **Spread:** 4–15' **Hardiness:** zones 4–11

Winter Jasmine

Jasminum

Winter jasmine is a great plant for winter interest. The green stems stand out against our gray winter background, and the bright yellow flowers bloom very early in the growing season.

Growing

Winter jasmine grows well in **full sun** or **partial shade**, in **moderate to fertile, well-drained** soil. This drought-tolerant plant adapts to most soil conditions.

When using winter jasmine in formal settings, prune out one-third of the oldest growth each year after flowering finishes.

J. nudiflorum (above & below)

Tips

The long, trailing stems of winter jasmine make an excellent groundcover. Rooting where the stems touch the ground, this tough plant forms large, dense colonies. It is very effective on hard-to-access slopes and in areas with less than ideal soils. Winter jasmine can also be grown in a shrub or mixed border; when it is planted in a container, the stems can trail over the sides.

Trained as a vine to grow on a trellis, winter jasmine can reach 15' or more in height.

Recommended

J. nudiflorum is a spreading, mounding, deciduous shrub with slender, arching to trailing, green stems. It grows 3–10' tall and spreads 4–10'. In winter and early spring, unscented, yellow flowers appear before the attractive, glossy, dark green foliage emerges. The foliage develops no fall color.

Features: slender, deciduous shrub; dark green foliage; yellow flowers; attractive habit **Height:** 3–10' or more **Spread:** 4–10' **Hardiness:** zones 6–9

Yucca
Yucca

Y. gloriosa cultivar

The leaves of Y. gloriosa *have smooth margins and are not as stiff (or as hazardous) as those of close relatives* Y. filamentosa *(Adam's needle) and* Y. aloifolia *(Spanish bayonet).*

This tough succulent makes a striking architectural statement in any garden. Whether planted alone or en masse, yucca makes an excellent low-maintenance addition to traditional and modern landscapes.

Growing
Yucca grows best in **full sun**, in **light, sandy, well-drained, neutral to slightly acidic** soil, but it adapts to most well-drained soils. Don't overwater, especially in winter, as plants do not tolerate soggy, cold soil.

Pruning is not needed, but the flower spikes can be removed when flowering is finished, and dead leaves can be removed as needed.

Tips
Yucca looks great as an accent plant in beds, borders and foundation plantings. It also looks good as a specimen in pots, planters and urns. The variegated varieties add color and texture to beds and borders.

Recommended
Y. gloriosa is an erect, slow-growing shrub. It has 24–36" long, sword-like, blue-green to dark green leaves that arise from a basal rosette. With age, the plant develops a thick trunk and loses its lower leaves. Older plants may also develop branches, with a rosette of foliage atop each branch. The fragrant, purple-tinged, white flowers are held above the foliage on tall, spike-like clusters. Cultivars are available.

Also called: Spanish dagger, mound-lily yucca
Features: rounded rosette of long, stiff, spiky, evergreen foliage; summer flowers; appealing habit **Height:** 4–6'; up to 8' when flowering
Spread: 4–6' **Hardiness:** zones 6–10

Belinda's Dream

Modern Shrub Rose

Belinda's Dream will provide you with successive flushes of fragrant, double, pink blossoms against blue-green, disease-tolerant foliage, resulting in an excellent landscape rose.

Growing

Belinda's Dream prefers **full sun** but tolerates late afternoon shade. The soil should be **well drained** and **moderately fertile**. Deadhead to encourage blooming. Keep overhead irrigation off the foliage. Prune in late winter to encourage a flush of spring blooms.

Tips

This modern shrub rose works well in mixed borders and is especially effective when planted in large groups, as low hedging or en masse. The large blooms make excellent cut flowers.

Recommended

Rosa **'Belinda's Dream'** is a shrub rose with characteristics of a hybrid tea, such as the high center bloom and long stem. It is a fast-growing shrub with a sturdy, upright habit, and it produces fully double, pink blossoms in repeat flushes.

Belinda's Dream is designated a Texas Earth-Kind® Rose by the Texas AgriLife Extension Service.

Features: fragrant, double, pink flowers; habit
Height: 4–5' **Spread:** 3–4' **Hardiness:** zones 5–9

Carefree Beauty

Modern Shrub Rose

Carefree Beauty was released in 1977, after it was found along Katy Road in Houston, Texas. It is a perfect choice for gardens that experience very hot, dry summers.

Growing

Carefree Beauty prefers **full sun** but tolerates late afternoon shade. While it is very disease tolerant, if planted in too much shade, this rose can experience fungal diseases. The soil should be **average to fertile, humus rich, slightly acidic, moist** and **well drained**, but Carefree Beauty has proven to be quite adaptable to a variety of soil conditions.

Carefree Beauty is designated a Texas Earth-Kind® Rose by the Texas AgriLife Extension Service.

Deadhead to encourage repeat blooming. Keep overhead irrigation off the foliage. Prune in late winter to encourage a flush of spring blooms.

Tips

Carefree Beauty makes a great addition to a mixed bed or border with perennials. It can also be mass planted to create a large display, and it is equally attractive as a specimen.

Recommended

Rosa 'Carefree Beauty' is a fast-growing, vigorous, medium-sized shrub that produces deep pink, single or semi-double blooms up to 4" in diameter in successive flushes from spring through fall. An abundance of large, orange hips follow.

Also called: Katy Road Pink **Features:** deep pink flowers; rounded habit; summer foliage; long blooming period; attractive, orange hips; disease tolerant **Height:** 5' **Spread:** 5' **Hardiness:** zones 4–9

Climbing Pinkie
Climbing Polyantha Rose

Climbing Pinkie was introduced in 1952. At only 10' tall, this climber can be grown in smaller spaces. Its dense, cascading habit makes it the perfect specimen climber.

Growing

Climbing Pinkie thrives in **full sun** with good air circulation. **Moderately fertile, well-drained, moist, humus-rich** soil is best. This rose can tolerate saline irrigation as long as soil is amended with organic matter. Keep irrigation water off the foliage. Remove old canes after flowering in late spring.

Tips

Climbing Pinkie can be used to cascade over retaining walls or trained to grow up trellises, arbors and pillars. It can also be trained to cover fences. Its mounding habit and size also allow you to use it as a natural hedge.

Recommended

Rosa 'Climbing Pinkie' is a fast-growing, vigorous, mounding climber with light green foliage and very few thorns. It bears semi-double, lightly fragrant, pink blooms primarily in spring, with some fall re-bloom possible.

Climbing Pinkie is designated a Texas Earth-Kind® Rose by the Texas AgriLife Extension Service.

Features: lightly fragrant, semi-double, pink blooms **Height:** 10' **Spread:** 7' **Hardiness:** zones 6–9

Knock Out

Modern Shrub Rose · Landscape Rose

Growing

Knock Out grows best in **full sun**. The soil should be **fertile, humus rich, slightly acidic, moist** and **well drained**. This rose blooms most prolifically in warm weather but has deeper red flowers in cooler weather. Deadhead lightly to keep the plant tidy and to encourage prolific blooming.

Tips

This vigorous rose makes a good addition to a mixed bed or border, and it is particularly effective when planted in groups of three or more. It can be mass planted to create a large display or grown singly as an equally beautiful specimen.

This rose has become a standard land-scaping rose owing to its tough con-stitution and ease of care. Knock Out tolerates conditions that many other roses won't, while still blooming prolifically.

Recommended

Rosa **'Knock Out'** has a lovely, rounded form with glossy, green leaves that turn to shades of burgundy in cool weather. The bright cherry red flowers are borne in clus-ters of 3–15 almost all summer long and even into fall. Orange-red hips last well into winter. **'Blushing Knock Out,' 'Double Knock Out,' 'Pink Knock Out'** and **'Sunny Knock Out'** are all available. However, these cultivars tend not to per-form as well as the original Knock Out.

Knock Out is designated a Texas Earth-Kind® Rose by the Texas AgriLife Extension Service. However, it is susceptible to disease.

Features: rounded habit; light, tea rose scented, midsummer to fall flowers in shades of pink and red; disease resistant **Height:** 4–5' **Spread:** equal to height **Hardiness:** zones 4–10

Marie Daly

Polyantha Rose

Marie Daly is a new variety of Marie Pavie, an old garden rose that dates back to 1888. Marie Pavie is a superb polyantha rose with white blossoms. The only difference between the two is Marie Daly's distinctly pink color.

Growing

Marie Daly prefers **full sun and moist, well-drained** soil, with adequate organic matter and humus. Marie Daly is an outstanding performer in almost any soil type, thriving in acidic and even highly alkaline soils.

Avoid overhead irrigation. Prune in late winter to encourage a flush of spring blooms.

Marie Daly is designated a Texas Earth-Kind® Rose by the Texas AgriLife Extension Service.

Tips

Marie Daly is one of the best roses for growing in a large container on a sunny patio or deck. Polyanthas typically produce small flowers in large clusters and are primarily used in containers and for planting en masse or grouped in mixed borders.

Recommended

Rosa '**Marie Daly**' has few thorns and produces successive flushes of very fragrant, semi-double to double, pink blooms from spring to frost. It also produces lush, bluish green foliage that is highly resistant to disease and pests.

Features: fragrant, semi-double to double, pink flowers **Height:** 3–4' **Spread:** 3–4' **Hardiness:** zones 5–9

Mutabilis

China Rose

This impressive rose produces a flurry of multi-colored blooms that resemble butterflies.

Growing

Mutabilis prefers locations in **full sun** but can tolerate some shade in the late afternoon. This rose thrives in hot, dry conditions. The soil should be **well drained** and **rich with organic matter** for best performance; however, you'll find this tough rose can tolerate varying soil conditions.

Once established, Mutabilis requires little care. Prune in late winter to encourage a flush of spring blooms, and then as needed in late summer to keep plant size under control. Provide ample space for this large shrub to spread.

Tips

Use this rose as a large specimen or anchor shrub at the back of mix beds. Its size also makes it a good choice for a natural hedge.

Recommended

Rosa **'Mutabilis'** is a large China rose with deep green foliage that emerges in shades of burgundy. A prolific bloomer, the flowers emerge yellow and change to pink, then a deep crimson, giving plants a multi-colored appearance. Mutabilis blooms continuously from spring through fall. This shrub is very tough and easy to grow.

Mutabilis is designated a Texas Earth-Kind® Rose by the Texas AgriLife Extension Service. It was introduced in 1894.

Also called: The Butterfly Rose **Features:** interesting, single flowers with a silky texture **Height:** 6' **Spread:** 6' **Hardiness:** zones 6–9

New Dawn
Climbing Rose

In 1910, Dr. William Van Fleet of the United States introduced a hybrid seedling named 'Dr. W. Van Fleet'; it gave rise to a repeat-blooming sport introduced in 1930 as 'The New Dawn.'

Growing

New Dawn grows well in **full sun** or **partial shade**, in **fertile, moist, well-drained** soil with at least **5% organic matter** mixed in. It has average watering needs once established, but avoid overhead irrigation.

Tips

Considered one of the easiest climbers to grow, New Dawn is suitable for pergolas, walls, fences, arches or pillars, or it can be pruned as a hedge or shrub. It is also a good rose for exhibition.

Recommended

Rosa 'New Dawn' is a vigorous, disease-tolerant climber with upright, arching canes that support abundant, medium to dark green, glossy foliage. Borne singly or in small clusters, the double flowers have a sweet apple fragrance and fade from a soft pink to a pinkish white.

New Dawn was celebrated as the world's first patented plant.

New Dawn is designated a Texas Earth-Kind® Rose by the Texas AgriLife Extension Service.

Also called: Everblooming, Dr. W. Van Fleet, The New Dawn **Features:** repeat blooming; pale pearl pink flowers from early summer to fall; climbing habit **Height:** 15–20' **Spread:** 10–15' **Hardiness:** zones 5–9

Perle d'Or

Polyantha Rose

Introduced in France 1884, Perle d'Or ("pearl of gold") is a tried and true performer in Texas gardens, even in heavy alkaline clay soil. It also tolerates our extreme heat and periods of drought.

Growing

Perle d'Or is very easy to grow in any landscape situation with **full sun** and good air circulation. It tolerates very hot direct sun and reflected heat. The soil should be **moderately fertile and well drained**. This rose tolerates a variety of soil conditions, but the addition of organic matter improves performance. Deadhead lightly as needed.

Tips

Perle d'Or is wonderful when grown in mixed perennial beds—salvias are especially good companions. Its size and shape also makes it perfect for large containers placed where you can enjoy the intense fragrance.

Recommended

Rosa **'Perle d'Or'** was bred in France by Dubreuil and is a cross between *R. polyantha* and 'Mme. Falcot'. It is a small, dense shrub and is one of the easiest to grow in Texas gardens. The double, pompon blooms emerge continuously from spring through fall. Apricot orange buds turn a golden buff pink as they open.

Perle d'Or is designated a Texas Earth-Kind® Rose by the Texas AgriLife Extension Service.

Features: highly fragrant, interesting flowers spring through fall; repeat blooming **Height:** 4' **Spread:** 4' **Hardiness:** zones 6–9

Spice
China Rose

This rose offers up a peppery fragrance, hence its name 'Spice.'

Growing

Spice needs **full sun** with good air circulation. The soil should be **well drained** and **organically rich**. Once established, it has average watering needs. Avoid overhead irrigation. Spice is generally disease tolerant, drought tolerant and easy to grow.

Tips

This medium-sized rose is a good landscaping shrub for less formal spaces. Use it as a specimen or in groups of 3 to 5 in mixed perennial beds. It can also be grown in large patio containers. It is an excellent cut flower for long-lasting indoor arrangements.

Recommended

***Rosa* 'Spice'** is a found rose of unknown parentage. It is believed it may actually be 'Hume's Blush Tea-Scented' China rose, which was introduced prior to 1810 and has borne many of the rose cultivars grown today. This small to medium shrub has an informal and sometimes twiggy growth habit. It produces successive flushes of double, white to light pink, fragrant blooms from spring through fall.

Spice is designated a Texas Earth-Kind® Rose by the Texas AgriLife Extension Service.

Features: white to light pink, double, fragrant flowers; repeat blooming **Height:** 5' **Spread:** 4' **Hardiness:** zones 7–9

The Fairy

Modern Shrub Rose

The Fairy is popular with both novice and experienced gardeners. It bears large clusters of dainty, rosette-shaped, soft pink, double flowers.

Growing

The Fairy grows well in **full sun** or **partial shade**; although it is prone to blackspot in partial shade, it will still bloom, with slower color fading. It prefers **fertile, moist, well-drained** soil with at least **5% organic matter** mixed in. The Fairy tolerates and even prefers neglect.

Tips

This rose can be used in containers, as a groundcover, in mixed beds and borders, as a weeping standard or left to trail over a low wall or embankment. It looks great massed or planted as low hedging. It makes a beautiful cut flower and is useful for covering a stump in the sun.

Recommended

Rosa 'The Fairy' is a compact, mounding plant with moderately prickly canes, glossy foliage and soft pink, double flowers. Trouble free and highly resistant to disease, it blooms continually from summer until fall frost.

The Fairy is designated a Texas Earth-Kind® Rose by the Texas AgriLife Extension Service.

Also called: Fairy, Feerie **Features:** repeat blooming; soft pink flowers from late summer to fall; low maintenance **Height:** 2'
Spread: 2–4' **Hardiness:** zones 4–9

Blue Sky Vine
Thunbergia

Blue sky vine is a stunning climber. Its late bloom time and huge, lavender blue, morning glory–like flowers make this vine a showstopper in any garden.

Growing

Blue sky vine performs best in **full sun** or **light shade**. Grow it in **fertile, well-drained** soil that is **high in organic matter**.

When temperatures dip below 25° F, this vine typically dies to the ground, but it will re-emerge when temperatures warm in spring.

Tips

Blue sky vine is a tenacious grower that requires support. Be sure to provide a sturdy trellis or fence. Add this vine to areas that need a burst of color in fall.

Recommended

T. grandiflora is a vigorous, twining climber with fleshy, green vines and large, leathery leaves. It bears large, blue to lavender flowers in late summer and fall. **Var. *variegata*** has variegated foliage.

T. grandiflora

Features: twining habit; large, light blue to lavender blue flowers; leathery, heart-shaped foliage **Height:** 20' **Spread:** 15' **Hardiness:** zones 8–11 (may be root hardy in zone 7)

Blue sky vine can be grown in large containers with a topiary frame and overwintered indoors to keep it evergreen.

Carolina Jessamine

Gelsemium

Carolina jessamine explodes into a cloud of yellow blooms in late winter and early spring. Plants may put on a repeat performance in fall. It is known to scamper up large trees, fences and even utility poles.

Growing

Carolina jessamine thrives in **full sun**. It can grow in partial shade but produces fewer flowers. The soil should be **moist, well drained** and **fertile**.

Pinch back the new growth to encourage a more dense growth habit. Cut it back to approximately 2–3' high when the growth is thin at the bottom and the top is falling over because of the weight. This vine should be pruned only immediately after flowering.

Tips

Carolina jessamine can be grown on a decorative trellis, pergola or arbor. It is often used to adorn mailboxes and just about anything that requires a bit of color and a vertical element.

This vine can also be used as an effective groundcover. For the best results, plant it in a place where it can be allowed to roam and won't be bothered once established.

Recommended

G. sempervirens is a vigorous vine that produces twining stems without the aid of tendrils. Masses of fragrant, funnel-shaped flowers are borne in late winter, in shades of golden to pale yellow. Dark, glossy foliage on rich brown stems is the perfect complement to the brightly colored blossoms.

G. sempervirens (above & below)

All parts of this plant are poisonous.

Features: bright yellow flower clusters; lush foliage; habit **Height:** 15–20' **Spread:** 4–5' **Hardiness:** zones 7–9

Clematis
Clematis

Clematis is a tough, low-maintenance climber that twines around nearby structures to provide privacy and beauty.

Growing

Clematis prefers **full sun** but tolerates partial shade. The soil should be **fertile, humus rich, moist** and **well drained**. Clematis requires regular watering during the first year to get established. Be sure to fertilize after blooming has finished.

This vine enjoys our warm climate, but its roots prefer to be cool. A thick layer of mulch or a planting of low, shade-providing perennials helps protect the tender roots. Provide shelter from winter winds.

Clematis blooms on the tips of the previous year's growth, so prune only after blooming has finished.

Tips

Clematis can climb up structures, such as trellises, railings, fences or sturdy arbors. It can also be allowed to grow over shrubs or up trees, or used as a groundcover.

Recommended

C. armandii (evergreen clematis) is a vigorous, evergreen climber that produces white, fragrant blooms in spring. The oblong, leathery foliage is an attractive dark green. A number of hybrids are available. **'Snowdrift'** is most common, while **'Apple Blossom'** offers pink buds and pale pink to white blooms. (Zones 5–9)

C. paniculata (above & below)

C. paniculata (*C. maximowicziana, C. terniflora;* sweet autumn clematis), one of the best *Clematis* species for Texas, is a vigorous, twining, deciduous or semi-evergreen vine that grows 15–20' tall. It has lush, deep green foliage. The fragrant, star-shaped, white flowers in late summer and early fall are followed by decorative seedheads. This vine self-seeds with much gusto and should be cut back if it's taking over. (Zones 4–8)

Many types of clematis are available in different forms and sizes, bearing a wide array of flower colors and bloom times.

Features: twining habit; fast-growing; spring or summer blooms; attractive foliage **Height:** 15–30' **Spread:** variable **Hardiness:** zones 4–9

Cross Vine

Bignonia

B. capreolata 'Jeckyll' (above & below)

This native vine is known to grow very large and at a rapid rate. It blooms like crazy and disguises unsightly surfaces and structures in no time.

Growing

Cross vine can tolerate a wide range of soil conditions but prefers **organically rich, well-drained** soil in **full sun, partial shade or light shade**.

Prune after flowering and whenever you find it necessary to train cross vine on its support.

Tips

This twining plant climbs up just about anything. The stems climb by holdfast disks at the end of their tendrils and rootlets, which act like little suction cups. When first planted, cross vine needs to be attached to the surface it will eventually climb.

Recommended

B. capreolata is a twining, vigorous vine that produces lush, green foliage along long, tough stems. Orange-yellow, tubular flowers with reddish throats emerge in spring and early summer. The foliage takes on a purplish red color as the days grow cooler in winter. Cultivars are available in other fiery colors as well.

Cross vine is sometimes confused with trumpet creeper. Although the two plants look somewhat similar, cross vine doesn't have the same invasive nature, and it blooms at a different time of the growing season.

Features: bright, fiery-colored flowers; vigorous, twining habit **Height:** 30–50' **Spread:** 20–40' **Hardiness:** zones 6–9

Honeysuckle

Lonicera

Honeysuckles can be rampant, twining vines, but with careful consideration and placement, they won't overrun your garden. The fragrance of the flowers makes any effort worthwhile.

Growing

Honeysuckle grows well in **full sun** or **partial shade**. The soil should be **average to fertile, humus rich, moist** and **well drained**.

Tips

Honeysuckle can be trained to grow up a trellis, fence, arbor or other structure. In a large container near a porch, it will ramble over the edges of the pot and up the porch railings with reckless abandon.

Recommended

There are dozens of honeysuckle species, hybrids and cultivars. Check with your local garden center to see what is available. The following is one of the more popular species.

L. sempervirens (trumpet honeysuckle, coral honeysuckle) bears orange or red flowers in late spring and early summer. Many cultivars and hybrids are available with flowers in yellow, red or scarlet, including the yellow-flowering '**John Clayton.**'

L. sempervirens 'Sulphurea' (above), *L. sempervirens* (below)

The nectar and flowers of honeysuckle are edible and have a honey-like flavor; however, the berries of most species are mildly poisonous and should not be consumed.

Features: creamy white, yellow, orange, red or scarlet, late spring and early summer flowers; twining habit; fruit **Height:** 6–12' **Spread:** 6–12' **Hardiness:** zones 4–9

Ivy
Hedera

H. helix (above & below)

One of the loveliest things about English ivy is the variation in green and blue tones it adds to the garden.

Growing

Ivy prefers **light shade** or **partial shade**. The soil should be of **average to rich fertility, moist** and **well drained**. The richer the soil, the better this vine grows. In a full sun or exposed site, the foliage can become damaged or dried out in winter.

Ivy can be invasive in warm climates. For slower growth, choose small-leaved cultivars. It's best not to allow ivy to grow up large trees, as it can weigh the tree down and cause damage.

English ivy is popular as a houseplant, and it is also frequently used in wire-frame topiaries.

Tips

Grown as a trailing groundcover, ivy roots at the stem nodes. As a climbing vine, it clings tenaciously to house walls, tree trunks, stumps and many other rough-textured surfaces, and the rootlets can damage walls and fences, so be careful.

Recommended

H. helix (English ivy) is a vigorous, evergreen plant with triangular, glossy, dark green leaves that may be tinged with bronze or purple in winter, thereby adding another season of interest to your garden. Many cultivars have been developed, including some with interesting, often variegated foliage. Check with your local garden center to see what is available. (Zones 5–9)

H. colchica (Persian ivy) is similar to English ivy, but with larger leaves and a higher tolerance to fungal leaf spot. Also more drought tolerant than English ivy, it's considered a superior choice for shady Texas gardens. It grows to 40' tall as a climbing vine. (Zones 6–11)

Features: attractive foliage; climbing or trailing habit
Height: 6–8" as a groundcover; up to 90' when climbing
Spread: indefinite **Hardiness:** zones 5–11

Passion Flower
Passiflora

Passion flower is mesmerizing. It is a fast-growing, woody climber with tendrils that is grown as a perennial vine. The unique flowers are a striking and create a tropical feel in the garden. Most passion flower varieties are native to North America.

P. incarnata (above), *P. caerulea* (below)

Growing

Grow passion flower in **full sun** or **partial shade**. This plant prefers **well-drained, moist** soil of **average fertility**. Keep it sheltered from wind and cold. In the more northern parts of the state, the vine may die down to the ground during winter, but re-emerge the following spring.

Fertilize passion flower sparingly. Too much nitrogen encourages lots of foliage but few flowers.

Tips

Passion flower is a popular addition to mixed containers and makes an unusual focal point near a door or other entryway. It is perfect for covering an unsightly fence or growing over an arbor.

Recommended

P. caerulea (blue passion flower) sports lovely white and blue flowers. It is best planted on a south-facing exposure to keep it from dying to the ground in winter. (Zones 8–10)

The plant is edible: the foliage tastes like peanut butter, and the small, round fruits are edible but not very tasty.

P. incarnata (maypops) is a vigorous, native climbing vine that produces tendrils to attach itself to a support. It has deeply lobed, ornate foliage and bowl-shaped, fragrant, pale purple to nearly white blossoms, with purple and white coronas, which are followed by yellow fruit.

There are many other species and cultivars available.

If you plant passion flowers, then the butterflies are sure to follow. Butterfly larvae often eat quite a bit of your passion flower foliage, but plants typically bounce back quickly.

Features: exotic flowers in a wide range of colors; some with edible fruit **Height:** 10–30' or more **Spread:** variable **Hardiness:** zones 6–10

Trachelospermum
Trachelospermum

T. jasminoides 'Variegatum'

These vines grow quickly to cover a trellis, arbor or fence or ground-cover area. They are evergreen except in harsh winters.

Confederate jasmine can also be used as an effective groundcover. For the best results, plant it where it can be allowed to roam and won't be bothered once established.

Growing

Trachelospermums do well in **full sun, partial shade** or **light shade**. They tolerate many soil conditions but prefer a **well-drained** soil. Once established, trachelospermums are very drought tolerant.

Plant Confederate jasmine about 36" apart, on southern exposures or close to the house for added protection from cold and wind. Place Asiatic jasmine plants approximately 12" apart for groundcover, and the area should be filled in completely in about two growing seasons.

Prune away any overgrown vines or dead leaves in late winter or early spring, before new growth emerges. Plants can be sheared if necessary, but avoid shearing regularly because the damaged leaf edges will show all season.

Tips

Confederate jasmine, with its pretty foliage and masses of fragrant blooms, is the perfect vine to place near a patio or deck. Asiatic jasmine is a tough, low-maintenance lawn substitute, especially in shady locations.

Recommended

T. asiaticum (Asiatic jasmine) is a creeping groundcover with small, dark green, leathery leaves. The stems are reddish brown. The small, yellow, star-shaped flowers are rarely seen.

T. jasminoides (Confederate jasmine, star jasmine) is a fast-growing vine with small, glossy, dark green leaves. Plants offer masses of highly fragrant, small, white, star-shaped flowers in spring. **'Madison'** is more compact, growing to only 12' tall, and more cold tolerant.

Features: fast-growing, evergreen vine; climbing or creeping habit; yellow or white, sometimes fragrant flowers; small, dark green foliage **Height:** 6–18" as groundcover; 12–40' as climbing vine **Spread:** variable **Hardiness:** zones 7–11

Trumpet Creeper
Campsis

C. radicans (above & below)

Trumpet creeper is a chugging locomotive of a plant that can cover just about any structure in less than five years. Its flowers help brighten the landscape and give it a lush feel.

Growing

This heat-tolerant vine flowers best in **full sun** but also grows well in partial shade or light shade. Growth is most rampant in **fertile** soil, but almost any soil will do.

Trumpet creeper needs frequent pruning to stay attractive and in bounds. Only plant it if you have lots of space for it to spread. You'll often find sprouts of trumpet creeper coming up quite a ways from the original plant. Once you have one of vigorous vines, you will probably never get rid of it.

Tips

Trumpet creeper clings to any surface—wall, tree, fence, telephone pole, etc.—but the aerial rootlets can damage painted surfaces. One plant can provide a privacy screen very quickly, or it can be grown up an exterior wall or over the porch of a house.

Recommended

C. radicans is a fast-growing, deciduous vine that climbs by aerial rootlets. It spreads by suckers and can form large, thick colonies. For a long period in summer, it bears trumpet-shaped, dark orange flowers. **'Crimson Trumpet'** has bright red flowers. **'Flava'** bears yellow flowers. **'Mme. Galen'** bears large, open, orange-red flowers.

Hummingbirds are attracted to trumpet creeper's long, tube-like flowers.

Also called: trumpet vine, hummingbird vine
Features: clinging habit; orange, red or yellow flowers; easy to grow **Height:** 30–40'
Spread: 30–40' **Hardiness:** zones 4–9

Virginia Creeper • Boston Ivy

Parthenocissus

P. quinquefolia (above & below)

Virginia creeper can cover the sides of buildings, helping to keep rooms cool in the summer heat. Cut the plants back to keep windows and doors accessible.

Virginia creeper and Boston ivy are handsome vines that establish quickly and provide an air of age and permanence, even on new structures.

Growing

These vines can grow in full sun but perform best in **light shade to full shade**. The soil should be **fertile** and **well drained**. The plants adapt to clay or sandy soils.

Tips

Virginia creepers do not require support because they have clinging rootlets that can adhere to just about any surface, even smooth wood, vinyl or metal. Give the plants lots of space and let them cover a wall, fence or arbor. They can also be used as groundcovers.

Recommended

P. quinquefolia (Virginia creeper, woodbine) has dark green foliage. Each leaf is divided into five leaflets, and they turn flame red in fall.

P. tricuspidata (Boston ivy) produces glossy, dark green foliage reminiscent of grape leaves. The foliage turns shades of orange and red in fall. This self-climber can grow quite tall in a short time.

Features: summer and fall foliage; clinging tendrils **Height:** possibly 30–50', but limited by the size of support **Spread:** equal to height **Hardiness:** zones 3–8

Wisteria

Wisteria

Loose clusters of purple hang like lace from the branches of wisteria. With prudent pruning, a gardener can create beautiful tree forms and attractive arbor specimens.

Growing

Wisteria grows well in **full sun** or **partial shade**. The soil should be of **average fertility, moist** and **well drained**. Too fertile a soil produces lots of vegetative growth but very few flowers. Avoid planting wisteria near a lawn where fertilizer may leach over to your vine.

Wisteria may send up suckers and can root wherever branches touch the ground. To keep wisteria blooming sporadically all summer, prune off flowering spikes as soon as the flowers fade. Wisteria will send out new blooming shoots until frost.

Tips

Wisteria requires something to twine around, such as an arbor or other sturdy structure. Select a permanent site; this vine doesn't like to be moved. It is best not to allow it to grow up large trees, as it can weigh the tree down and cause damage.

Features: blue, purple, pink or white flowers; foliage; twining habit **Height:** 20–30' or more **Spread:** 20–30' or more **Hardiness:** zones 6–9

W. frutescens 'Amethyst Falls' (above), *W. macrostachya* 'Aunt Dee' (below)

Recommended

W. frutescens (American wisteria) is a twining climber clothed in divided leaves composed of 9–15 leaflets. Pea-like, fragrant flowers are borne in pendulous, lilac clusters. The flowers are followed by smooth, green seedpods, 4" in length. Cultivars are available with lilac blue or white flowers.

W. macrostachya (Texas wisteria, Kentucky wisteria) is a Texas native. It is very similar to American wisteria in appearance, but the flowers produced by this species are twice as long, reaching 12" lengths. Cultivars are available.

All parts of this plant are poisonous.

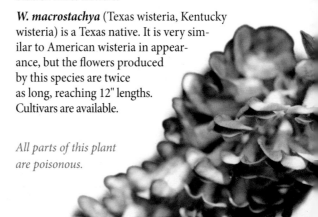

Blue Grape Hyacinth
Muscari

M. armeniacum (above & below)

Because grape hyacinth foliage persists through winter, this species can be planted as a marker around other bulbs to ensure that they aren't forgotten and inadvertently dug up.

Blue grape hyacinths are among the flowers that signal the emergence of spring. These tough bulbs are the perfect accompaniment to other spring bulbs; they contrast beautifully with just about any color combination.

Growing

Blue grape hyacinths prefer **full sun** or **partial shade**. The soil should be **moist, well drained** and **organically rich**. Plant the bulbs 4" deep in fall.

Tips

Blue grape hyacinths are great for naturalizing under shrubs and trees, and they look best when planted in clusters. They can be used in low-maintenance and low-water plantings and in mixed perennial beds. Blue grape hyacinths look beautiful planted with perennials that will slowly envelop the tired-looking grape hyacinth foliage as they fill in.

Recommended

M. armeniacum has showier, larger blooms than other *Muscari* species. It naturalizes very well in our Texas soil and climate.

M. botryoides is a compact form that produces grass-like foliage and clusters of urn-shaped, blue flowers atop 12" tall, slender green stalks. The flowers emit a strong, musky scent. It must be replanted every few years.

Also called: common grape hyacinth **Features:** grape-like clusters of fragrant, purple to blue flowers; attractive habit **Height:** 6–12" **Spread:** 6–8" **Hardiness:** zones 3–8

Caladium
Caladium

The foliage of caladiums is striking. If you are searching for bold texture for your shady garden, caladiums are a reliable choice.

Growing

Caladiums prefer **partial to full shade**, though a few sun-tolerant selections are available. They like **moist, well-drained, humus-rich, slightly acidic** soil.

Caladiums are grown for their foliage and planted as tubers. Make sure the knobby side of the tuber is facing up and is level with, or just under, the soil surface. The tubers prefer being planted in warm soil, ideally 70° F at a minimum; they may rot in cooler soil. You can purchase your tubers in mid-spring, but wait until after Mother's Day to plant them out.

C. bicolor cultivar (above), C. bicolor 'Sweetheart' (below)

Dig tubers in fall after the leaves die back. Remove as much soil as possible and let them dry for a few days. Store them in slightly damp peat moss at 55°–60° F. Or, simply purchase new tubers in spring.

Tips

Caladiums provide a tropical feel to your garden. They do very well around water features and in woodland gardens. They are equally effective in herbaceous borders en masse or as specimens and are wonderful plants for containers. When grown in containers, there is no need to dig the tubers in fall. Simply bring the whole container inside over winter.

Recommended

C. bicolor (*C. × hortulanum*) is native to the edge of woodlands in South America. The often-tufted, arrow-shaped foliage is dark green and is variously patterned with red, white, pink, green, rose, salmon, silver or bronze. Each leaf is 6–12" long. Many varieties and sizes are available.

All parts of caladium may irritate the skin, and ingesting this plant causes stomach upset.

Features: ornate, patterned, colorful foliage; habit; form **Height:** 18–24" **Spread:** 18–24" **Hardiness:** treat as an annual

Canna

Canna

C. hybrid (above & below)

Cannas are stunning, dramatically large foliage plants that give an exotic flair to any garden.

Growing

Cannas grow best in **full sun** in a sheltered location. The soil should be **fertile, moist** and **well drained**.

Plant out in spring after the chance of frost has passed and the soil has warmed. Cannas can be started early indoors to get a head start on the growing season. Deadhead to prolong blooming.

In areas of Texas where they are not cold hardy, the rhizomes can be lifted after the foliage is killed back in fall. Clean off any clinging dirt and store the rhizomes in a cool, frost-free location in slightly moist peat moss. Check on them regularly during winter, and if they start to sprout, pot them and move them to a bright window until they can be moved outdoors.

Tips

Cannas can be grown in a mixed perennial bed, or to fill in areas you want to keep low-maintenance. They make dramatic specimen plants and can even be included in large planters.

Recommended

A wide range of cannas is available, including cultivars and hybrids with green, bronzy, purple or yellow-and-green-striped foliage. Dwarf cultivars that grow only 18–28" tall are also available.

Canna flowers are a favorite of hummingbirds.

Features: decorative foliage; white, red, orange, pink, yellow and bicolored summer flowers **Height:** 18"–6' **Spread:** 20–36" **Hardiness:** zones 7–9

Crinum Lily

Crinum

Crinum lilies are a southern favorite, not only for their impressive, fragrant blooms, but also for their tenacity in the most unfavorable of growing conditions. If there was ever a "set it and forget it" plant, this is it.

Growing

Crinum lilies are best planted in **full sun** but can tolerate some late afternoon shade. While they prefer a **rich** soil, crinums will often grow quite happily in poor, compacted, clay soils. Be sure to plant the bulbs so that the neck is below the surface of the soil.

Crinum lilies will bloom repeatedly through summer; simply snip off spent blooms at the base of the stem, and new ones will follow.

Tips

Plant crinum lilies in a location where they can settle in long term. It's pretty tough to transplant them once they've dug in.

Recommended

C. bulbispermum is the most prolific and abundant species in the South. The foliage is blue-green, and the blooms range from pure white to pink with dark pink accents. Many varieties are available.

C. cultivar

C. × herbertii (milk and wine lily) is one of the first *Crinum* hybrids to bloom every summer and one of the toughest. It gives off a slight fragrance from white and pink blooms.

C. powelii is a tough, reliable species that puts on large quantities of rich pink flowers in summer. Many hybrids of this species are available.

Features: fragrant, trumpet-shaped, lily-like flowers; sturdy stems; strap like foliage **Height:** 24–36" **Spread:** 24–36" **Hardiness:** zones 7–10

Crinums are incredibly tough once established and will require little care or attention to thrive.

Daffodil

Narcissus

N. hybrid (above & below)

Many gardeners automatically think of large, yellow, trumpet-shaped flowers when they think of daffodils, but there is a wide range of color, form and size among the many varieties. In Texas, it's often the smaller-cupped daffodils that best naturalize.

A good general rule to know how deeply to plant bulbs is to measure the bulb from top to bottom and multiply that number by three.

Growing

Daffodils grow best in **full sun** or **light shade**. The soil should be **average to fertile** and **well drained**.

Bulbs should be planted in fall, 3–10" deep, depending on the size of the bulb—the bigger the bulb, the deeper it should be planted. Because our soil temperatures can get so warm in summer, it's often good practice to plant daffodil bulbs a little deeper, rather than too shallow.

Do not cut or mow the leaves until they turn yellow. Fertilize at planting time and each fall with a bulb food.

Tips

Daffodils are often planted where they can be left to naturalize, in the light shade beneath a tree or even in lawns. In mixed perennial beds, the summer foliage of other plants hides the faded daffodil leaves.

Recommended

Many species, hybrids and cultivars of daffodils are available. There are 13 divisions of daffodils based on flower form and heritage categories. For long-term naturalizing, choose large-cupped and small-cupped types rather than trumpet-type daffodils. **Jonquilla** hybrids are especially suited to our heavy soils, heat and humidity.

Features: white, yellow, peach, orange, pink or bicolored, spring flowers **Height:** 4–24" **Spread:** 4–12" **Hardiness:** zones 3–9

Hardy Amaryllis
Hippeastrum

When it comes to tolerating low temperatures and poor soils, this is the amaryllis that tops the rest. Believed to be the first hybrid amaryllis, this tough beauty has become a favorite in southern gardens.

Growing

This is not your common florist's amaryllis typically used for indoor forcing. These hardy bulbs tolerate our heat, humidity and even areas with heavy clay soils. Plants can be grown in **full sun** but also happily tolerate partial shade.

Plant the bulbs with their "necks" just above the surface of the soil. Blooms will emerge first in spring and then are followed by the foliage. Do not cut or remove foliage while it is still green. The bulbs go dormant in fall, after which the foliage will die away.

H. hybrid

Tips

Plant hardy amaryllis in large clumps in mixed perennial beds, groundcover areas or in natural plantings under trees that provide afternoon shade.

Recommended

H. × johnsonii is known for its bright crimson blooms striped with white, followed by long, strap-like foliage.

Also called: Johnson's amaryllis, St. Joseph's lily
Features: red-and-white-striped, trumpet-shaped, spring flowers; long, strap-like foliage; slight fragrance **Height:** 10–24" **Spread:** 6–8" **Hardiness:** zones 7–10

Hardy amaryllis was hybridized and made available to gardeners some time during the 1700s.

Iris

Iris

I. sibirica (above), *I. germanica* 'Stepping Out' (below)

Divide in late summer or early fall depending on the species. Only replant clean, disease- and insect-free rhizomes. Deadhead irises to keep them tidy.

Tips

Use irises in borders. Yellow and blue flag irises are also useful alongside streams or ponds. Dwarf cultivars make attractive additions to rock gardens.

Wash your hands after handling irises because they can cause severe internal irritation if ingested.

Recommended

Many iris species and hybrids are available. Among the most popular is the **bearded iris**, often a hybrid of **I. germanica**. It has the widest range of flower colors. **I. cristata** (dwarf crested iris) is a low-growing, native species that bears multi-colored flowers. **I. fulva** (copper iris) bears copper blooms. **I. orientalis** (spuria iris) is reliable and offers vanilla-scented blooms. **I. pallida** (Dalmatian bearded iris) bears amethyst blooms in April. **I. pseudoacorus** (yellow flag, Louisiana iris) is a water dweller and tolerates wet locations where little else thrives. **I. sibirica** (Siberian iris) offers assorted cultivars with flowers in a variety of shades, including purple, blue and white. **I. versicolor** (blue flag) produces blooms in shades of light to dark violet-blue, but cultivars are available in shades of red, pink and reddish purple.

All irises are popular border plants. The range of colors for bearded irises approximates that of a rainbow.

Growing

Irises prefer **full sun** but tolerate light shade. The soil should be of **average fertility, moist** and **well drained**. Bearded iris tolerates dryer soils and should not be over-watered. Yellow flag prefers very moist soil and can even be grown in standing water.

Ask for remontant (reblooming) iris cultivars for flowers in spring and again in fall.

Features: spring, summer and sometimes fall flowers in almost every color combination including bicolored and multi-colored; attractive foliage **Height:** 4"–4' **Spread:** 6"–4' **Hardiness:** zones 3–10

Oxblood Lily
Rhodophiala

While often hard to find, this rare bulb is an incredibly tough and reliable fall bloomer in southern gardens.

Growing

Oxblood lily thrives just about anywhere in the state and in varying growing conditions. Plant it in **full sun** or **partial shade**; the flowers will last longer if they receive some shade in the afternoon. Oxblood lily thrives in heat, humidity and **poor** soils. It is very drought tolerant and can be used in low-maintenance and low-water gardens.

Plant bulbs at a depth that is approximately three times the height of the bulb. If you have bulbs with very long necks, you can leave a portion of the neck above the soil.

R. bifida

Tips

Oxblood lily can be mixed into groundcover beds, lawns or perennial beds and will multiply year after year.

Recommended

R. bifida is a tough, reliable bulb. Plants produce unscented, trumpet-shaped, deep red flowers in fall, followed by strap-like foliage that remains through spring.

Features: deep red flowers in fall; strap-like foliage in winter; easy to grow **Height:** 12–24" **Spread:** variable as clump spreads **Hardiness:** zones 7–10

Native to Argentina, this beautiful bulb was brought to Texas by German settlers.

Rain Lily
Zephyranthes

Z. candida (above & below)

Sometimes, the most delicate looking flowers can be the toughest. Rain lilies are known for bursting into bloom just after a rain shower in spring and summer.

Growing

Rain lilies grow well in **full sun** or **partial shade**. They tolerate a variety of soil conditions, although they prefer **well-drained** soil. They are very drought tolerant once established. Plants will appreciate annual applications of compost in heavier clay soils.

Rain lilies are very easy to grow from seed; the seeds are produced often and ripen in about four weeks.

There are cultivars available that provide a varying range of colors, such as 'Prairie Sunset,' which blooms in peach.

Tips

Rain lilies are excellent for mixing into perennial or groundcover beds in clumps. They can also easily be grown in containers.

Recommended

Z. candida bears pure white blooms with a green throat. It is one of the toughest species available.

Z. citrine (*Z. sulfurea*) is the most common of the yellow-blooming species. It spreads easily by seed.

Z. grandiflora has lavish pink blooms, 3" across. The largest and showiest of the rain lilies, it prefers rich soil and regular feeding. It may sometimes be offered mistakenly as *Z. robusta*, another pink-blooming species.

Features: white, pink, yellow or bronze, tubular flowers that emerge after rain; thin, grass like, clumping foliage; prolific seed production **Height:** 8–12" **Spread:** 8–12" but clumps vary **Hardiness:** zones 7–10

Spider Lily
Lycoris

Spider lily is named for its out-stretched stamens that resemble the legs of an arachnid.

Growing

Spider lilies prefer **full sun**, with some late afternoon shade. **Fertile, moist, well-drained** soil is best. Mulching is recommended for moisture conservation.

Plant the bulbs in late summer or fall about 12" apart, with the bulb necks just above the soil surface. To prevent rot, select an area that remains mostly dry during the bulbs' summer dormancy. Some water is tolerated if there is excellent drainage. Propagation by division should take place only once the plants have stopped blooming for the season.

Tips

Spider lilies can be planted in mixed perennials beds, established in lawns and planted in ground-cover beds. They are perfect for naturalizing in woodland areas that receive at least morning sun.

Recommended

L. radiata (red spider lily) is a classic red heirloom that sends up foliage and blooms in fall. The foliage is dormant in summer. *L. aurea* is a less common yellow species, and *L. albiflora* produces white flowers.

L. squamigera (pink spider lily, magic lily, surprise lily, hurricane lily, resurrection lily, naked lady) is a cold-hardy, bulbous perennial that forms clusters of fragrant,

L. squamigera (above), *L. radiata* (below)

funnel-shaped, pale rosy red flowers made up of slightly wavy petals with curved tips. Long, wiry stamens emerge from the center of each flower. Strap-shaped leaves are produced each spring.

The heirloom strain of L. radiata *is a triploid bulb (it has an extra set of chromosomes), which make it especially tough. However, modern-day imports are typically diploid and less vigorous.*

Features: red, yellow, white and pink, spider-like flowers **Height:** 18–24" **Spread:** 12–18"
Hardiness: zones 6–10

Spring Star Flower

Ipheion

'Alba' (above), *I. uniflorum* (below)

What is more representative of a new spring season than a blooming, bulbous perennial with wildflower appeal? Spring star flower is unique and is deserving of wider use throughout the South.

Growing

Spring star flower grows well in **full sun** or **partial shade**. It performs well in almost any **well-drained** soil.

To plant spring star flower in lawns, use a trowel to lift a small piece of turf and insert the bulb; replace the patch of turf. It's that easy.

The bulbs should be planted approximately 2" deep and 2" apart from one another in fall. Division is unnecessary because the plants become more attractive as they multiply into larger clumps.

Tips

Spring star flower is ideal for naturalizing in lawns and woodlands. You can also plant spring star flower in groups around the base of larger-growing bulbs and perennials.

Recommended

I. uniflorum is a vigorous, clump-forming perennial that emerges from a bulbous root. It produces narrow, strap-like foliage and single flowers with overlapping petals. The flowers are often a pale silvery blue. Many cultivars with scented, white, deep violet or lilac blue flowers are available at your local garden center.

Features: star-shaped, fragrant, colorful flowers; habit **Height:** 6–8" **Spread:** 4–6" **Hardiness:** zones 6–9

Summer Snowflake

Leucojum

Of you wish you could grow lily of the valley but have had little success, summer snowflake is a good alternative. Although it doesn't offer an intense fragrance, the dangling, white blooms create a similar look.

Growing

Summer snowflakes can be planted in **full sun** or **light shade**. They thrive in **organically rich, well-drained** soil but will adapt to clay soil. Once established, these drought-tolerant bulbs require little to no irrigation to thrive.

Plant the bulbs about twice the depth of the height of the bulb. Just as with daffodils, allow the foliage to mature after the spring bloom season. Do not remove it until it begins to turn yellow. Their need for a hot, dry dormant summer season makes them the perfect choice for low-maintenance Texas gardens.

L. aestivum (above), 'Gravetye Giant' (below)

Tips

Summer snowflakes are tough bulbs perfect for naturalizing in Texas gardens. They are especially good for naturalizing under deciduous trees. You can also plant them in clumps in mixed perennial beds.

Do not confuse summer snowflake with snowdrops, which are species in the genus Galanthus. Snowdrops do not perform well in our Texas heat and humidity.

Recommended

L. aestivum bears pendulous, pure white, bell-shaped flowers with green tips in late winter and early spring. The dark green foliage is grass like, similar to daffodils. Cultivars are available.

Features: bell-shaped, white, late winter and early spring flowers; dark green, grass-like foliage
Height: 12–18" **Spread:** approximately 12"
Hardiness: zones 4–8

Chives

Allium

A. schoenoprasum (above & below)

The delicate onion flavor of chives is best enjoyed fresh. Mix chives into dips or sprinkle them on salads and baked potatoes.

Chives are said to increase appetite and encourage good digestion.

Growing

Chives grow best in **full sun**. The soil should be **fertile, moist** and **well drained**, but chives adapt to most soil conditions. These plants are easy to start from seed, but they do like the soil temperature to stay above 65° F before they germinate, so seeds started directly in the garden are unlikely to sprout before late spring or early summer.

Tips

Chives are decorative enough to be included in a mixed or herbaceous border and can be left to naturalize. In an herb garden, chives should be given plenty of space to allow self-seeding.

Recommended

A. schoenoprasum forms a clump of bright green, cylindrical leaves. Clusters of pinkish purple flowers are produced in early and midsummer. Varieties with white or pink flowers are available.

Chives spread recklessly as the clumps grow larger and the plants self-seed.

Features: foliage; form; white, pink or pinkish purple flowers **Height:** 8–24" **Spread:** 12" or more **Hardiness:** zones 3–9

Cilantro • Coriander

Coriandrum

Cilantro is a multi-purpose herb—its leaves and seeds each have distinct flavors and are common ingredients in South Asian, South American and many other types of cuisine. The leaves are called cilantro and are used in salads, salsas and soups; the seeds are called coriander and are used in pies, chutneys and marmalades.

Growing

These plants prefer **full sun** but tolerate partial shade. The soil should be **fertile, light** and **well drained**. They are low maintenance.

Cilantro is grown as a cool-season herb in Texas because it does not tolerate our summer heat. Begin planting in early fall and again in late winter or early spring. By late spring, plants begin to go to seed. Harvest leaves fall through spring. Harvest seeds in late spring. Cilantro dies soon after it goes to seed with the return of warm weather.

Tips

Cilantro has pungent leaves with a flavor that you'll either love or hate. Add a plant or two here and there throughout your borders and vegetable garden, both for visual appeal and to attract beneficial insects. It is excellent for containers.

Recommended

C. sativum forms a clump of lacy basal foliage above which large, loose clusters of tiny, white flowers are produced. The seeds ripen in late spring.

C. sativum (above & below)

Allow your plants to flower before pulling them from the garden. The delicate, cloud-like clusters of flowers attract pollinating insects, such as butterflies and bees, as well as an abundance of predatory insects that help keep pest insects at a minimum in your garden.

Features: form; foliage; white flowers; seeds
Height: 18–24" **Spread:** 8–18" **Hardiness:** frost-hardy, cool-season annual in Texas

Dill

Anethum

A. graveolens (above & below)

Dill leaves and seeds are probably best known for their use as pickling herbs, though they have a wide variety of other culinary uses.

Growing

Dill grows best in **full sun** but will tolerate some afternoon shade. The soil should be of **poor to average fertility, moist** and **well drained**.

Dill is grown as cool-season herb in Texas because it does not tolerate our summer heat. Plant it in fall. Harvest leaves fall through spring, and harvest seeds in late spring and early summer.

Tips

With its feathery leaves, dill is an attractive addition to a mixed perennial bed or border. It can be included in a vegetable garden but does well in any sunny location. It is excellent in containers.

Recommended

A. graveolens forms a clump of feathery foliage. Clusters of large, yellow flowers are borne at the tops of sturdy stems.

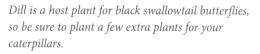

Dill is a host plant for black swallowtail butterflies, so be sure to plant a few extra plants for your caterpillars.

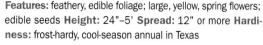

Dill turns up frequently in historical records as both a culinary and medicinal herb. It was used by the Egyptians and Romans and is mentioned in the Bible.

Features: feathery, edible foliage; large, yellow, spring flowers; edible seeds **Height:** 24"–5' **Spread:** 12" or more **Hardiness:** frost-hardy, cool-season annual in Texas

Fennel
Foeniculum

Fennel is a beautiful, aromatic herb. Its stalks, leaves and fruit, which all have an anise-like flavor, are used for both culinary and medical purposes. It is one of the primary ingredients in absinthe. Bulbing forms are used more as a vegetable.

Growing

Fennel grows best in **full sun** but will tolerate some afternoon shade. The soil should be of **poor to average fertility, moist** and **well drained**.

Fennel is grown as cool-season herb in Texas because it does not tolerate our summer heat. Harvest stalks and leaves from fall through spring; harvest seeds in late spring and early summer. Harvest Florence fennel bulbs when they reach the size of a tennis ball.

Tips

With its feathery leaves, fennel is an attractive addition to a mixed perennial bed or border. It can be included in a vegetable garden but does well in any sunny location. It is excellent in containers.

Recommended

F. vulgare forms a clump of fine, feathery foliage. Clusters of large, yellow flowers are borne at the tops of sturdy stems. **Var. *azoricum*** (Florence fennel) forms a large, bulb-like structure at the base

'Purpureum' (above), *F. vulgare* (below)

of the plant. While the flavor is still anise-like, it is milder and sweeter. Plants tend to be smaller, and the bulb-like section is harvested and prepared like a vegetable. **'Purpureum'** ('Nigra'; bronze-leafed fennel) makes a stunning ornamental plant in the garden with other cool-season annuals.

If you plan to harvest seed for re-planting, dill and fennel should not be grown close together. They will cross-pollinate, and the seeds of both plants will lose their distinct flavors.

Features: feathery, edible foliage; large, yellow, spring flowers; edible seeds **Height:** 24"–5' **Spread:** 12" or more **Hardiness:** frost-hardy, cool-season annual in Texas

Lemon Balm

Melissa

M. officinalis (above & below)

The leaves can be harvested fresh or dried for teas, both hot and cold. They are also useful for flavoring desserts and savory dishes.

This lemon-scented and lemon-flavored herb is indispensable to cooks who love a touch of lemon in most dishes.

Growing

Lemon balm prefers to grow in **full sun** but grows quite successfully in locations with light shade. The soil should be **moist, fertile** and **well drained**, but this plant can tolerate poor, dry soils.

Taking cuttings for culinary use encourages dense, vigorous growth. It's best to remove the flowers as they emerge.

Tips

Lemon balm, a relative of mint, can be invasive may spread throughout your garden if not contained. Herb gardens are often the preferred location for this useful perennial, but it also works well as a fragrant filler in containers.

Recommended

M. officinalis is a bushy, dense-growing perennial with roughly textured, hairy leaves that are fragrant and flavorful when bruised or crushed. Flowers are produced but are inconspicuous and should be removed to keep the plant vigorosly producing leaves.

Features: fragrant, useful foliage
Height: 24" **Spread:** 18–24"
Hardiness: zones 3–7

Mint
Mentha

The cool, refreshing flavor of mint lends itself to tea and other hot or cold beverages. Mint sauce, made from freshly chopped mint leaves, is often served with lamb.

Growing

Mint grows well in **full sun** or **partial shade**. The soil should be **average to fertile, humus rich** and **moist**. This plant spreads vigorously by rhizomes and may need a barrier in the soil to restrict its expansion.

Tips

Mint is a good perennial groundcover for damp spots. It grows well along ditches that may only be periodically wet. It also can be used in beds and borders, but place mint carefully because it may overwhelm less vigorous plants. Plant it in containers to control spread.

M. × piperita 'Chocolate' (above), M. × piperita citrata (below)

A few sprigs of fresh mint added to a pitcher of iced tea give it an extra zip.

Recommended

There are many species, hybrids and cultivars of mint. **M. spicata** (spearmint), **M. × piperita** (peppermint) and **M. × piperita citrata** (orange mint) are three of the most commonly grown culinary varieties. There are also more decorative varieties with variegated or curly leaves, as well as varieties with unusual, fruit-scented leaves.

The flowers attract bees, butterflies and other pollinators to the garden.

Features: fragrant foliage; purple, pink or white, summer flowers **Height:** 6–36" **Spread:** 36" or more **Hardiness:** zones 4–8

Oregano • Marjoram
Origanum

Oregano and marjoram are two of the best known and most frequently used herbs. They are popular in stuffings, soups and stews, and no pizza is complete until it has been sprinkled with fresh or dried oregano leaves.

Growing
Oregano and marjoram grow best in **full sun**. The soil should be of **poor to average fertility, neutral to alkaline** and **well drained**. Oregano is very tough and is easy to grow in Texas. Harvest leaves throughout the growing season.

Tips
These bushy perennials make a lovely addition to any perennial bed and can be trimmed to form low hedges. They are also excellent for trailing over retaining walls.

Recommended
O. majorana (marjoram) is upright and shrubby with light green, hairy leaves. It bears white or pink flowers in summer. (Zones 7–9)

O. vulgare **var.** *hirtum* (oregano, Greek oregano) is the most flavorful culinary variety of oregano. The low, bushy plant has hairy, gray-green leaves and bears white flowers. Many other interesting varieties of *O. vulgare* are available, including those with golden, variegated or curly leaves.

O. vulgare 'Aureum' (above & below)

The flowers attract pollinators to the garden.

Features: fragrant, edible foliage; white or pink, summer flowers; bushy, semi-evergreen habit
Height: 12–32" **Spread:** 8–18" **Hardiness:** zones 4–9

Parsley

Petroselinum

*A*lthough parsley is usually used as a garnish, it is rich in vitamins and minerals and is reputed to freshen the breath after garlic- or onion-rich foods are eaten.

Growing

Parsley grows well in **full sun** or **partial shade**. The soil should be of **average to rich fertility, humus rich, moist** and **well drained**. Plants are tough, pest free and easy to grow with little care.

Parsley is grown as a cool-season herb in Texas because it does not tolerate our summer heat. Direct seed or plant out in early fall through early spring. Harvest the leaves fall through spring.

P. crispum (above), *P. crispum* var. *crispum* (below)

Tips

Containers of parsley can be kept close to the house for easy picking. The bright emerald green leaves are quite eye-catching in the middle of winter. Parsley is an excellent companion for other cool-season ornamentals such as pansies and violas.

Recommended

P. crispum forms a clump of bright green, divided leaves. This plant is a biennial but is usually grown as an annual because the leaves are the desired parts, not the flowers or the seeds. Cultivars may have flat or curly leaves. Flat leaves are more flavorful and curly are more decorative. Dwarf cultivars are also available.

Parsley is an excellent plant for butterfly gardens as a larval food source for swallowtails.

Features: attractive, edible foliage **Height:** 8–24"
Spread: 12–24" **Hardiness:** frost-hardy, cool-season annual in Texas

Rosemary

Rosmarinus

R. officinalis (above & below)

Rosemary is a beautiful evergreen shrub that produces tiny flowers sporadically throughout the year. The needle-like leaves are used to flavor a wide variety of culinary dishes, including chicken, pork, lamb, rice, tomato and egg dishes.

Growing

Rosemary thrives in hot, **full sun** conditions. The soil should be **well drained** and of **poor to average fertility**.

Rosemary is one of the toughest and easiest to grow landscaping plants in Texas. Plants become small evergreen shrubs that can be harvested from year-round. You may need to provide winter protection in the more northern parts of the state.

Tips

Rosemary is often grown as a shrub in low-maintenance and low-water plantings in Texas. Low-growing, spreading varieties can be planted along the top of a retaining wall or in containers.

Recommended

R. officinalis is a dense, bushy, evergreen shrub with narrow, dark green leaves. The habit varies somewhat between cultivars from strongly upright to prostrate and spreading. Many cultivars are available. Flowers are usually in shades of blue, but pink-flowered cultivars are available.

Because rosemary can produce flowers during times of year when most other plants are not in bloom, it is a helpful food source for bees.

Features: fragrant, evergreen foliage; bright blue or sometimes pink flowers throughout the year **Height:** 8"–4' **Spread:** 12"–4' **Hardiness:** zones 8–10

Sage
Salvia

Sage is perhaps best known as a flavoring for stuffing and dressing, but it has a great range of uses and is often included in soups, stews, sausages and dumplings.

Growing

Sage prefers **full sun** but tolerates late afternoon shade. The soil should be of **average fertility** and **well drained**. These plants benefit from a light mulch of compost each year. They are drought tolerant once established.

Tips

Sage is an attractive plant for a border, adding volume to the middle of the border or as an attractive edging or feature plant near the front. Sage can also be grown in mixed containers.

Recommended

S. officinalis is a woody, mounding plant with soft, gray-green leaves. Spikes of light purple flowers appear in early and midsummer. Many cultivars with attractive foliage are available, including the

'Icterina' (above), 'Purpurea' (below)

silver-leaved **'Berggarten,'** the purple-leaved **'Purpurea,'** the yellow-margined **'Icterina'** and the purple, green and cream variegated **'Tricolor,'** which has a pink flush to the new growth.

Sage has been used since at least ancient Greek times as a medicinal and culinary herb and continues to be widely used for both those purposes today.

Features: fragrant, decorative foliage; blue or purple, summer flowers **Height:** 12–24" **Spread:** 18–36" **Hardiness:** zones 5–8

Sweet Basil

Ocimum

'Genovese' (above & below)

The sweet, fragrant leaves of fresh basil add a delicious, licorice-like flavor to salads and tomato-based dishes.

Growing

Sweet basil grows best in a warm, sheltered location in **full sun**. The soil should be **fertile, moist** and **well drained**.

Plant out or direct sow seed after frost danger has passed in spring. Pinch the tips regularly to encourage bushy growth. Harvest the leaves regularly throughout the growing season.

Tips

Although sweet basil grows best in a warm spot outdoors in the garden, it can be grown successfully indoors in a pot by a bright window to provide you with fresh leaves year-round.

Recommended

O. basilicum is one of the most popular of the culinary herbs. There are dozens of varieties, including ones with large or tiny, green or purple and smooth or ruffled leaves.

Sweet basil is a good companion plant for tomatoes—both like warm, moist growing conditions, and when you pick tomatoes for a salad you'll also remember to include a few sprigs of basil.

Also called: basil **Features:** fragrant, decorative leaves **Height:** 12–24" **Spread:** 12–18" **Hardiness:** tender annual

Thyme
Thymus

Thyme is a popular culinary herb used in soups, stews and casseroles, and with roasts. It also makes for an excellent landscaping plant as a groundcover, stepping stone plant or edging plant.

Growing

Thyme prefers **full sun**. The soil should be of **poor to average fertility, neutral to alkaline** and very **well drained**. It is beneficial to work compost and expanded shale into the soil. Do not overwater; plants that sit in wet soil or receive too much irrigation will die out.

Once thymes finish flowering, shear them back by about one-half to encourage new growth and prevent them from becoming too woody.

Tips

Thymes work well at the front of borders, between or beside paving stones, in rock gardens, on rock walls and in containers. Creeping thyme makes a good lawn substitute for areas with reduced foot traffic.

Recommended

T. × citriodorus (lemon-scented thyme) forms a mound of lemon-scented, dark green foliage with pale pink flowers. Cultivars with silver- or gold-margined leaves are available.

T. praecox **subsp.** *arcticus* (*T. serpyllum*; mother of thyme, creeping thyme, wild thyme) is a low-growing variety with purple flowers. Many cultivars are available. **'Elfin'** forms tiny, dense mounds of foliage. **'Lanuginosis'** (wooly thyme) is a mat-forming selection with fuzzy, gray-green leaves and pink or purple flowers.

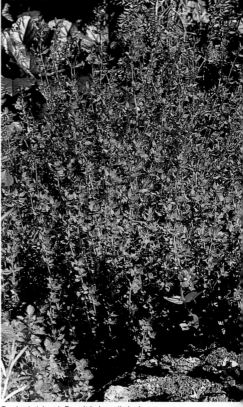

T. vulgaris (above), *T. × citriodorus* (below)

T. vulgaris (common thyme) forms a bushy mound of dark green leaves and purple, pink or white flowers. Cultivars with variegated leaves are available.

Thymes help keep the herb garden evergreen.

Features: bushy habit; fragrant, decorative foliage; purple, pink or white flowers **Height:** 2–12" **Spread:** 4–16" **Hardiness:** zones 4–8

Big Bluestem
Andropogon

A. gerardii (above & below)

Big bluestem is an integral part of prairie grassland restorations.

This native grass is found growing naturally in almost every state and was historically a prominent part of both tall- and short-grass prairies. Although it is no longer as prevalent in its native habitat, it will shine in any Texas garden.

Growing

Big bluestem prefers to grow in **full sun**. The soil should be **light, low in fertility** and very **well drained**.

This ornamental grass has a considerable tolerance for drought conditions, and excessive moisture can be a detriment. However, plants grown with little water often remain shorter in height and more compact in form than plants grown with adequate moisture.

Tips

The colorful foliage and flowerheads are a great addition to the back of a mixed perennial and shrub border. Big bluestem also works well in a naturalized garden setting.

Recommended

A. gerardii forms into a dense clump of arching, bluish green leaves that grow up to 5' in length or more and turn bronze in fall. Erect stems supporting deep red-purple flowers emerge in fall, followed by distinctive three-branched seedheads.

Features: colorful foliage, flowers and seedheads; form; habit **Height:** 4–6' **Spread:** 2–3'
Hardiness: zones 4–10

Blue Oat Grass
Helictotrichon

H. sempervirens (above & below)

This hardy grass is the perfect plant for those who desire a super-sized version of blue fescue for their garden.

Growing

Blue oat grass thrives in **full sun**. The soil should be **average to dry** and **well drained**. This grass is considered to be an evergreen but still needs a trim in spring to encourage new growth and simply to tidy it up.

Tips

Blue oat grass is ideal for just about any setting because of its versatility. It works well in a water-wise design or a naturalized area. It is a lovely complement to flowering perennials and shrubs because of its color, overall size and growth habit.

Recommended

H. sempervirens is a large, non-spreading grass that produces perfectly rounded, dome-shaped clumps of intensely blue, blade-like leaves. Wiry, tan stems tipped with tan seedheads emerge through the foliage.

Blue oat grass is easily propagated by division in early spring.

Features: brilliant blue foliage; decorative, spiked seedheads **Height:** 24–36" **Spread:** 24–30"
Hardiness: zones 3–8

Feather Reed Grass

Calamagrostis

'Overdam' (above), 'Karl Foerster' (below)

Feather reed grass may be susceptible to rust in cool, wet summers or in areas with poor air circulation.

This graceful, metamorphic grass changes its habit and flower color throughout the seasons. The slightest breeze keeps feather reed grass in perpetual motion.

Growing

Feather reed grass grows best in **full sun**. The soil should be **fertile, moist** and **well drained**. Heavy clay and dry soils are tolerated.

Rain and heavy snow may cause feather reed grass to flop temporarily, but it quickly bounces back. Cut it back to 4–6" in early spring before growth begins, and divide it when it begins to die out in the center.

Tips

Whether it's used as a single, stately focal point, in small groupings or in large drifts, feather reed grass is a desirable, low-maintenance grass. It combines well with late summer- and fall-blooming perennials.

Recommended

C. × acutiflora '**Karl Foerster**' (Foerster's feather reed grass) is the most popular selection and forms a loose mound of green foliage from which airy bottlebrush flowers emerge in June. The flowering stems have a loose, arching habit when they first emerge but grow more stiff and upright over summer. Other cultivars include '**Overdam**,' a compact, less hardy selection with white leaf edges. Watch for a new introduction called '**Avalanche**,' which has a white center stripe.

Features: open habit becomes upright; silvery pink flowers turn rich tan; green foliage turns bright gold in fall; winter interest **Height:** 3–5' **Spread:** 2–3' **Hardiness:** zones 4–9

Fountain Grass

Pennisetum

Fountain grass' low-maintenance needs and graceful form make it easy to place. It softens any landscape, even in winter.

Growing

Fountain grass thrives in **full sun**. The soil should be of **average fertility** and **well drained**. Plants are drought tolerant once established. They may self-seed but are not troublesome. Shear back perennial selections in early spring, and divide them when they start to die out in the center.

Tips

Fountain grass can be used as an individual specimen plant or in group plantings and drifts, or it can be combined with flowering annuals, perennials, shrubs and other ornamental grasses. Annual selections are often planted in containers or beds for height and stature.

P. setaceum 'Rubrum' (above & below)

Recommended

P. alopecuroides is a popular perennial clumping species. It is one of the most reliable and showy of the ornamental selections. It bears glossy, bright green foliage 24–36" tall and wide. Cooler temperatures in fall bring out the streaked yellow and brown leaf variegations from base to tip. The foliage fades to a straw color in winter. Showy flowers emerge in summer and persist into fall. **'Hameln'** is a dwarf variety that grows to only 24" tall.

P. setaceum (annual fountain grass) has narrow, green foliage and pinkish purple flowers that mature to gray. Its cultivar **'Rubrum'** (red annual fountain grass) has broader, deep burgundy foliage and pinkish purple, sterile flowers. There are a number of new cultivars on the market that offer larger foliage, flowers and plant sizes.

Both perennial and annual fountain grasses exist.

Features: arching, fountain-like habit; silvery pink, dusty rose to purplish black foliage; white or pinkish purple flowers; winter interest
Height: 12–36" **Spread:** 12–36" **Hardiness:** zones 6–10 for perennial species

Grama

Bouteloua

B. curtipendula (above), B. gracilis (below)

Grama is a Texas native forage grass that is gaining popularity as an ornamental grass for low-maintenance gardens and landscapes.

Growing

Gramas are best suited to **full sun** in **dry, well-drained** soil. Newly planted specimens will need supplemental water to get established, but mature plants will easily drown with regular irrigation. Gramas have an expansive root system that makes them very drought tolerant.

Cut foliage down to several inches above the crown in late winter before new growth emerges.

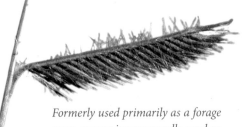

Formerly used primarily as a forage grass, grama is now usually used as an ornamental.

Tips

Grama performs well in sunny, rocky areas with other species that require little maintenance. It can also be used as a turf grass kept mowed to 2–4".

Recommended

B. curtipendula (side oats grama) is a long-lived, warm-season, native grass with a wide distribution throughout the United States. It grows to 36" tall. Bright red blooms occur along one side of the seed stalk. The mature seeds droop from this one edge; thus the name.

B. gracilis (blue grama) is a more compact species with fine leaves and blue-green seedheads. It grows to only 10–12" tall and wide.

Features: blue-green foliage with reddish bronze fall color; small, red flowers along sides of seed stalk **Height:** 10–36" **Spread:** 10–24" **Hardiness:** zones 3–9

Indian Grass

Sorghastrum

Indian grass is a beautiful prairie grass with a shimmering golden effect to its flowers. It is a valuable livestock foraging grass as well as a useful ornamental.

Growing

Indian grass prefers to grow in **full sun**. Although tolerant of poor conditions and soil types, Indian grass prefers to grow in **deep, rich, moist, loamy** soils. This species is drought tolerant once established. It does not tolerate excessive winter moisture.

Tips

Indian grass is often most effective in mass plantings and restoration sites or when naturalizing. It's also ideal for erosion control on slopes and provides a reliable show year-round, whether as a single specimen, a background grass or an accent in a mixed bed.

Recommended

S. nutans is a spreading perennial grass with an upright, clumping form. It bears foliage in shades of light to medium green, gray-green or pale shades of bluish green. The leaf blades are very narrow and gently arch out from the center. Yellowish tan flowers are borne in summer and are displayed as light, feathery plumes until the following spring. The foliage turns yellow to burnt orange in fall. Cultivars are available.

S. nutans 'Sioux Blue' (above & below)

Indian grass can range in height and spread depending on soil depth and moisture level.

Features: reliability; habit; color
Height: 3–5' **Spread:** 2–3'
Hardiness: zones 4–9

Inland Sea Oats
Chasmanthium

C. latifolium (above & below)

The flower stalks of inland sea oats, which resemble strings of dangling fish, make interesting additions to fresh or dried arrangements.

This native grass is at home in moist, shady woodlands, and its bamboo-like foliage gives it a tropical flair.

Growing

Inland sea oats thrives in **full sun to full shade**; however, to avoid leaf scorch in full sun, the soil must stay moist, and in deep shade, the upright, cascading habit relaxes. The soil should be **fertile** and **moist**, but dry soils are tolerated.

To deal with the vigorous self-seeding, deadhead in fall or pull the easily removed seedlings for sharing with friends or composting. Divide to control the rapid spread. Cut this plant back each spring to 2" above the ground.

Tips

Inland sea oats is a tremendous plant for moist, shady areas. Its upright to cascading habit, especially when in full bloom, is attractive alongside a stream or pond, in a large drift or in a container. However, plants do reseed, so be prepared for this grass to spread.

Recommended

C. latifolium forms a spreading clump of bamboo-like, bright green foliage. The scaly, dangling, spikelet flowers arrange themselves nicely on delicate stems, just slightly above the foliage. The foliage sometimes turns bronze, and the flowers turn gold in fall. **'River Mist'** has variegated foliage.

Also called: northern wood oats, Indian wood oats, spangle grass **Features:** bamboo-like foliage; unusual flowers; winter interest **Height:** 32"–4' **Spread:** 18–24" **Hardiness:** zones 5–8

Little Bluestem

Schizachyrium

Little bluestem offers year-round interest. This ornamental grass has graceful, swaying blades in spring and summer, followed by tall flower spikes in summer that evolve into fluffy plumes of seedheads that catch the light.

Growing

Little bluestem requires **full sun** and is tolerant of almost any soil type except those with inadequate drainage; the soil must be **well drained**. This ornamental plant is known to self-seed readily. Propagate it by both seed and division.

Tips

Little bluestem is a welcome addition to xeriscape gardens and naturalized areas. It also works well in mixed borders and more contemporary settings.

Recommended

S. scoparium is a clump-forming grass. It produces light green, narrow, blade-like leaves 12–16" in length that become darker with maturity. The leaves are of a medium texture, somewhat hairy and soft to the touch. Flower spikes emerge through the foliage, supported by stems that rise high above the leaves. Decorative, fluffy plumes of ripening seedheads range in color from bronze to bright orange. 'Blaze' is similar in form but displays more intense fall color, from reddish purple to orangey pink.

S. scoparium (above & below)

Little bluestem is drought tolerant but benefits from a little summer watering in more arid regions.

Also called: prairie beard grass **Features:** form; habit; decorative foliage and seedheads; winter interest **Height:** 2–4' **Spread:** 1–3' **Hardiness:** zones 3–8

Maiden Grass
Miscanthus

'Strictus' (above), 'Zebrinus' (below)

The mature height of your maiden grass selection will determine the best place for it in the border.

Maiden grass is one of the most popular and majestic of all the ornamental grasses. Its graceful foliage dances in the wind and makes an impressive sight all year long.

Growing
Maiden grass prefers **full sun**. The soil should be of **average fertility, moist** and **well drained**, though some selections tolerate wet soil. All selections are drought tolerant once established.

Leave the foliage in place to provide winter interest and then cut it back in spring before the new growth starts.

Tips
Give this magnificent beauty room to spread so you can fully appreciate its form. Maiden grass creates a dramatic impact in groups or as a seasonal screen.

Recommended
M. sinensis has many cultivars, all distinguished by the white midrib on the leaf blade. Some popular selections include **'Gracillimus,'** with long, fine-textured leaves; **'Grosse Fontaine,'** a tall, wide-spreading, early flowering selection; **'Morning Light'** (variegated maiden grass), a short, delicate plant with fine, white leaf edges; **var. *purpurascens*** (flame grass), with foliage that turns bright orange in early fall; **'Strictus'** (porcupine grass), a tall, stiff, upright selection with unusual horizontal yellow bands; and **'Zebrinus'** (zebra grass), an arching grass with horizontal yellow bands on the leaves. **'Adagio'** is a dwarf selection that keeps to 3' tall and is perfect for smaller spaces.

Also called: eulalia, Japanese silver grass **Features:** upright, arching habit; colorful summer and fall foliage; pink, copper or silver, late summer and fall flowers; winter interest **Height:** 3–10' **Spread:** 2–5' **Hardiness:** zones 5–8; zone 4 with protection

Muhly Grass
Muhlenbergia

Looking at the pinkish purple haze of the flower plumes of muhly grass, you may think you're witnessing some kind of unusual atmospheric phenomenon.

Growing

Muhly grass thrives in **full sun**, but it tolerates light shade. It prefers **well-drained, moist** soil. Once established, muhly grass prefers dryer soil that is well aerated; however, it is tolerant of just about any soil type.

Muhly grass is known to self-seed. If you want thicker stands, leave the ripened seedheads in place and allow the seeds to fall. Otherwise, remove the seedheads before they ripen.

Tips

This wild-looking, medium-sized grass is suited to mixed beds and borders with bolder-leaved plants that bring attention to its delicate appeal. It's also useful for naturalizing areas of your garden that require little attention or care and works well as a groundcover in areas with poor soil.

Recommended

M. capillaris (*M. filipes*; gulf muhly grass, mist grass, hairy awn muhly grass, pink muhly grass) produces a dense, knee-high stand of fine, wispy, grayish green grass. This showy clump can grow 3–4' tall and wide. Purplish flowerheads emerge in late summer and last for up to two months. '**Regal Mist**' bears rosy pink flowers. '**White Cloud**' has white flowers.

M. capillaris (above & below)

M. lindheimeri (Lindheimer muhly grass) is a clumping grass bearing 12–18" tall, bluish green blades that gently arch toward the ground. Upright, spike-like flowers emerge in shades of purple from fall into winter and float 18–24" above the foliage.

The fall color stands out while most other plants look spent.

Features: form; purple seedheads in fall **Height:** 3–4' **Spread:** 3–4' **Hardiness:** zones 5–10

Sedge
Carex

C. comans 'Frosted Curls' (above), C. buchananii (below)

Sedge foliage comes in green, blue, rust, bronze or gold, which allows the gardener to add broad strokes of color to the landscape.

Growing

Most sedges grow well in **full sun** or **partial shade** in **moist, well-drained, neutral to slightly alkaline** soil. 'Frosted Curls' prefers average to dry soil and is drought tolerant once established.

Stems can be cut to the ground in early spring before new growth occurs, or they can be "combed" to remove the older foliage. Propagate sedges by seed or division of clumps in mid-spring to early summer.

Tips

Use these plants in rock gardens, water features, containers and borders. The fine foliage of 'Frosted Curls' contrasts well with coarse-textured plants.

Recommended

There are many sedges available. **C. buchananii** (leatherleaf sedge) is a densely tufted, evergreen perennial with an arching habit and orange-brown foliage; **C. comans 'Frosted Curls'** (*C.* 'Frosted Curls'; New Zealand hair sedge) is a compact, clump-forming, evergreen perennial with fine-textured, very pale green, weeping foliage that appears almost iridescent and has unusual curled and twisted tips; **C. grayi** (Gray's sedge) has star-like seedheads and clumps of rich green leaves; **C. plantaginea** (seersucker sedge) has showy flowers and bright green leaves with many veins; **C. siderosticha 'Variegata'** (striped broad-leaved sedge) resembles a mass of narrow, 1" wide hosta leaves. **C. texensis** is a native commonly found in central Texas.

"Sedges have edges," the opening line to a classic gardener's poem, points out that sedges, unlike true grasses, have triangular stems.

Features: interesting, colorful foliage; growth habit **Height:** 6–36" **Spread:** 24–36" **Hardiness:** zones 5–9

Switch Grass

Panicum

A native of the prairie grasslands, switch grass naturalizes equally well in an informal border and a natural meadow.

Growing

Switch grass thrives in **full sun, light shade** or **partial shade**. The soil should be of **low fertility** and **well drained**, though this grass adapts to moist or dry soils and tolerates conditions ranging from heavy clay to lighter sandy soil.

The flower stems may break under heavy, wet snow or in exposed, windy sites. Cut switch grass back to 4–6" from the ground in early spring.

Tips

Plant switch grass singly in small gardens or in large groups in spacious borders or at the edges of ponds or pools for a dramatic, whimsical effect. The seedheads attract birds, and the foliage changes color in fall, so place this plant where you can enjoy both features.

Recommended

P. virgatum is suited to wild meadow gardens. It comes in both blue and red varieties. Some of its popular blue cultivars include **'Heavy Metal,'** an upright plant with narrow, steely blue foliage flushed with gold and burgundy in fall, and **'Prairie Sky,'** an arching plant with deep blue foliage. **'Shenandoah'** is a small, compact selection with red-tinged, green foliage that turns burgundy in fall.

P. virgatum cultivar (above), 'Heavy Metal' (below)

Switch grass' delicate, airy panicles fill gaps in the garden border and can be cut for fresh or dried arrangements.

Features: clumping habit; green, blue or burgundy foliage; airy panicles of flowers; fall color; winter interest **Height:** 3–5' **Spread:** 30–36" **Hardiness:** zones 3–9

Athyrium

Athyrium

A. niponicum var. pictum (above), *A. felix-femina* (below)

This genus of ferns includes some of the best-behaved ferns; they add color and texture to shady spots without growing out of control.

Growing

Lady ferns and Japanese painted ferns grow well in **full shade, partial shade** or **light shade**. The soil should be of **average fertility, humus rich, acidic** and **moist**. Division is rarely required but can be done to propagate more plants.

Tips

Both ferns form an attractive mass of foliage, but they don't grow out of control like some ferns tend to. Include them in shade gardens and moist, woodland gardens.

The colorful foliage of Japanese painted fern brightens up any shaded area with its metallic shades of silver, burgundy and bronze.

Recommended

A. felix-femina (lady fern) forms a dense clump of lacy fronds. It grows 12–24" tall and has a 24" spread. Cultivars are available, including dwarf cultivars and cultivars with variable foliage. **Subsp.** *asplenioides* (southern lady fern) is a native form with more triangular fronds.

A. niponicum var. *pictum* (Japanese painted fern) forms a clump of dark green fronds with a silvery or reddish metallic sheen. It grows 12–24" tall and has a 24" spread. Many cultivars are available. Some of the more colorful cultivars include '**Burgundy Lace**,' with metallic burgundy leaves; '**Metallicum**,' with variegated silver, green and red leaves; '**Pewter Lace**,' with fine, metallic gray foliage and '**Ursula's Red**,' with iridescent, silver-white and rich maroon-red leaves. (Zones 4–8)

Features: habit; foliage **Height:** 12–24"
Spread: 12–24" **Hardiness:** zones 3–8

Autumn Fern
Dryopteris

D. erythrosora (above & below)

Autumn fern is a reliable, hardy, eye-catching fern that is easy to grow. New growth emerges with tones of copper and bronze, providing excellent foliage color contrast.

Growing

Autumn fern grows best in **partial shade**, preferably morning sun with shade in the afternoon. It tolerates deep shade with very little loss in vigor. The soil should be **fertile, humus rich, moist** and **well drained**. Divide the plant in spring to control its spread and to propagate.

Tips

This large, impressive fern is useful as a specimen or grouped in a shaded area or woodland garden. It is ideal for an area that stays moist but not wet, and it beautifully complements other shade-loving plants, including hostas and coral bells.

Recommended

D. erythrosora is an upright, evergreen perennial fern with large, slightly arching, bronzy green to dark green fronds. The new growth has a bronzy red hue. The large, red spore structures on the undersides of the fronds are conspicuous. If an extreme late frost kills the plant to the ground, it will recover and send up new growth.

The genus Dryopteris is made up of 225 species of moisture-loving ferns native to shady woodlands in temperate regions around the world.

Also called: Japanese red shield fern, wood fern
Features: decorative fronds and habit **Height:** 24–36" **Spread:** 24–36" **Hardiness:** zones 5–9

Blunt-Lobed Wood Fern

Woodsia

W. obtusa (above & below)

This small, native fern is often found growing on rock ledges and cliffs throughout the eastern U.S. It is a perfect addition to a shady rock wall or woodland garden.

Growing

Blunt-lobed wood fern prefers **partial shade** and **fertile** soil that is **well drained** and consistently **moist**.

Tips

This fern is ideal for woodland gardens, shade gardens and natural or introduced rocky outcrops, including rock gardens and rock walls.

Recommended

W. obtusa is a small fern with deeply cut fronds that have a very lacy appearance. This species slowly creeps by rhizomes, ultimately reaching a spread of 18". It remains compact in a mounding form.

Every state in the U.S. has at least one native species of Woodsia. *They hybridize easily, so many variations occur naturally.*

Also called: blunt-lobed woodsia **Features:** ornate foliage; habit **Height:** 18–24" **Spread:** 12–18" **Hardiness:** zones 4–10

Christmas Fern

Polystichum

Christmas fern is native to a large swath of the east coast from Canada to Florida, and inland to the Mississippi River. Of the hardy ferns, it is one of the lower growing specimens.

Growing

Christmas fern grows well in **partial to full shade**. The soil should be **fertile, humus rich** and **moist**.

Divide this fern in spring to propagate more plants or to control its spread if it gets out of bounds. Dead and tired-looking fronds should be removed in spring before the new ones fill in.

P. acrostichoides (above & below)

Tips

Christmas fern can be used in beds and borders and is a good choice for a shaded, pond-side garden. It is better suited to moist rather than wet conditions. The use of the fronds as Christmas decorations gave the plant its common name. Christmas fern is mostly deer proof.

Recommended

P. acrostichoides (Christmas fern) is a vase-shaped, evergreen perennial fern that forms a circular clump of arching, dark green, lance-shaped fronds. Fertile fronds are shorter and slightly wider than the sterile fronds.

P. polyblepharum (Japanese tassel fern, bristle fern) is an evergreen species with 12–30" long, arching fronds. This ornate fern can spread up to 36" wide. (Zones 5–8)

This genus of evergreen ferns provides greenery year-round, and the appearance of the fronds varies significantly from species to species.

Features: evergreen foliage; easy to grow; problem free **Height:** 12–32" **Spread:** 18–36" **Hardiness:** zones 3–9

Cinnamon Fern

Osmunda

O. cinnamomea (above), O. regalis (below)

Ferns have a certain prehistoric mystique and can add a graceful elegance and textural accent to your garden.

Growing

Cinnamon ferns prefer **partial shade** or **light shade** but tolerate some direct sun if the soil is consistently moist. The soil should be **fertile, humus rich, acidic** and **moist**; they tolerate wet soil. Cinnamon ferns will spread as offsets form at the plant bases.

Tips

These large ferns form an attractive mass when planted in large colonies. They can be included in beds and borders and make a welcome addition to a woodland garden or the edge of a pond.

The royal fern's "flowers" are actually its conspicuous, spore-producing sporangia.

Recommended

O. cinnamomea (cinnamon fern) has light green fronds that fan out in a circular fashion from a central point, with the whole plant resembling a large badminton birdie. Bright green, leafless, fertile fronds that mature to cinnamon brown are produced in spring and stand straight up in the center of the plant.

O. regalis (royal fern, flowering fern) forms a dense clump of foliage. Feathery, flower-like, fertile fronds stand out among the sterile fronds in summer and mature to a rusty brown.

Features: deciduous perennial fern; decorative fertile fronds; habit **Height:** 2–5' **Spread:** 2–4' **Hardiness:** zones 3–9

Japanese Holly Fern
Cyrtomium

C. falcatum

Japanese holly fern is a coarse-textured, heat-tolerant, easy-to-grow plant that provides a wonderful contrast to lacy-textured plants in shady spots. It can take drier conditions than many ferns and is deer resistant.

Growing

Japanese holly fern grows well in **partial to full shade**, in **fertile, moist, well-drained** soil with a lot of organic matter mixed in. This fern often grows best when it is not pampered. It tolerates some drought and should not be overwatered—keep the soil just moist during the growing season.

Tips

Use Japanese holly fern in shaded beds and borders, in rock gardens, at the edges of woodland gardens and in containers. Japanese holly fern also makes a great houseplant in reasonably bright rooms. Its glossy, dark green foliage provides winter interest.

Recommended

C. falcatum is an evergreen perennial fern with slender, arching stems that grow up from erect, scaly rhizomes. It has shiny, leathery, dark green fronds with holly-like pinnae (fern leaflets). Dwarf cultivars and cultivars with variations in the foliage are available.

Japanese holly fern is a great container plant indoors or out, and the attractive, long-lasting fronds can be cut for use in flower arrangements.

Features: evergreen perennial fern; attractive fronds; decorative habit; low maintenance
Height: 24–36" **Spread:** 24–36" **Hardiness:** zones 6–10

Sensitive Fern

Onoclea

O. sensibilis (above & below)

A common sight along stream banks and in wooded areas in its native habitat, sensitive fern thrives in moist, shaded conditions.

Growing

Sensitive fern grows best in **light shade** but tolerates full shade or partial shade. The fronds can scorch if exposed to too much sun. The soil should be **fertile, humus rich** and **moist**, though some drought is tolerated.

Tips

Sensitive fern likes to live in damp, shady places. Include it in shaded borders, woodland gardens and other locations with protection from the wind.

Recommended

O. sensibilis forms a mass of light green, deeply lobed, arching fronds. Fertile fronds are produced in late summer and persist through winter. The spores are produced in structures that look like black beads, giving the fertile fronds a decorative appearance that makes them a popular addition to floral arrangements. **'Texas Too Tall'** is a variety that will grow to 36" tall, about 12" taller than the standard species.

Sensitive fern is sensitive to frost and can be easily damaged by late and early frosts.

Features: deciduous perennial fern; attractive foliage; habit **Height:** 24–36"
Spread: indefinite **Hardiness:** zones 4–9

Southern Wood Fern

Thelypteris

Ferns generally prefer the shadier parts of a garden, but southern wood fern can tolerate sunnier and dryer conditions than many other ferns.

Growing

Southern wood fern grows well in **light shade** or **partial shade** but can tolerate a fair amount of direct sun as long as the soil remains moist. The soil should be of **average fertility, humus rich, slightly acidic** and **moist**. This fern grows adequately in hot, dry conditions but is most impressive in moist, shaded locations.

T. kunthii (above & below)

Divide the plants regularly or pull up extra plants to control the vigorous spread. Cut out crusty old foliage in spring before new growth begins.

Tips

This fern makes an attractive addition to a shaded garden or to the edge of a woodland garden. It is best used where there is plenty of room for it to spread. The light green foliage provides contrast against darker green plants.

Recommended

T. kunthii (*T. normalis*) is a deciduous perennial fern that spreads by rhizomes and spores. Where it is happy, it spreads quickly. This fern has large, trianglar, gently arching, light green fronds and white stems. The fronds are not frost hardy.

This lovely fern spreads quickly and is useful for filling lightly shaded locations.

Also called: Kunth's maiden fern, southern shield fern, widespread maiden fern **Features:** foliage; fast growth; easy to maintain **Height:** 12–36" **Spread:** 24–48"
Hardiness: zones 7–10

Bugleweed

Ajuga

'Catlin's Giant' (above & below)

Often labeled as a rampant runner, bugleweed grows best where it can roam freely. It provides colorful, low-growing foliage and beautiful blue flowers.

Growing

Bugleweed develops the best leaf color in **partial shade** or **light shade** but tolerates full shade. The leaves may become scorched when exposed to too much sun. Any **well-drained** soil is suitable.

Divide these vigorous plants any time during the growing season. Remove any new growth or seedlings that don't show the hybrid leaf coloring.

Tips

Bugleweed makes an excellent groundcover for difficult sites, such as exposed slopes and dense shade. It is also attractive in shrub borders.

Recommended

A. reptans is a low, quick-spreading groundcover. The many cultivars are grown for their colorful, often variegated foliage. Look for '**Burgundy Glow**,' '**Catlin's Giant**' and '**Variegata**,' just to name a few.

Bugleweed's dense growth prevents the spread of all but the most tenacious weeds.

Features: purple, blue, pink or white, late spring to early summer flowers; colorful foliage **Height:** 3–6" **Spread:** 24–36" **Hardiness:** zones 3–9

Hardy Plumbago
Ceratostigma

C. plumbaginoides (above & below)

This creeping perennial is not only easy to grow, but it also offers up beautiful blue flowers in summer.

Growing

Hardy plumbago grows best in **full sun** but survives with partial shade. It prefers **moist, well-drained** soil that is **rich in organic matter**. It is moderately drought tolerant once established. Divide in spring.

Tips

This quick-growing plant makes an excellent and tough groundcover. Hardy plumbago also makes a wonderful addition between rocks, under high-canopy trees, trailing from retaining walls or containers or planted along walkways.

Recommended

C. plumbaginoides is a woody plant with erect stems. The foliage, which starts out light green highlighted with purple and becomes darker green as the outdoor temperature rises, turns bronzy red in fall.

True blue flowers in the garden are few and far between.

Also called: leadwort **Features:** blue flowers; attractive habit; fall color **Height:** 7–12" **Spread:** 24–36"
Hardiness: zones 5–8

Lily Turf
Liriope

L. muscari (above), 'Variegata' (below)

Lily turf is an excellent groundcover plant that grows so thick that weeds can't compete. It is very easy to grow, easy to obtain and relatively problem free.

Growing

Lily turf can be grown in full sun, but prefers to grow in **partial shade** or **light shade**, in **moderately fertile, humus-rich, moist, well-drained** soil. However, you'll find that it adapts to heavy clay soils just fine.

Once established, plants are tough as nails and will require little care to thrive. To encourage new growth, trim or remove winter-damaged foliage in late winter or early spring.

Not a true grass, lily turf is actually a member of the lily family.

Tips

Lily turf can be used as a dense groundcover and for erosion control. It looks great when planted in mass drifts and reduces the amount of mulch needed each year. Lily turf grows well under large deciduous trees, and it does well in containers.

Recommended

L. muscari is a slow-spreading, clump-forming, evergreen perennial that has wide, arching, grass-like, dark green foliage. The spikes of late summer, violet purple to white flowers are held above the foliage. Persistent, shiny, black or white berries follow. **'Big Blue'** has large, showy, lavender blue flowers, and plants produce larger, taller clumps. **'Variegata'** has lavender purple flowers; its foliage has creamy yellow edges.

Also called: monkey grass, border grass
Features: strap-like foliage; easy to grow; purple to white flowers **Height:** 12–18" **Spread:** 6–12"
Hardiness: zones 6–10

Mondo Grass

Ophiopogon

Mondo grass is an excellent groundcover, accent and contrast plant. The foliage displayed by black mondo grass is the perfect dark background to highlight any brightly colored plant or flower.

Growing

Mondo grass prefers to grow in **partial shade** or **light shade** in **moist, moderately fertile, well-drained, humus-rich** soil. The foliage is at its best in partial shade.

Mondo grass appreciates a thick mulch in winter in zones 5 and 6 but should otherwise be left uncovered. Remove foliage from the previous season before growth begins in late winter or early spring. Divide in spring just as new growth resumes.

O. planiscapus 'Nigrescens' (above), *O. japonicus* 'Bluebird' (below)

Tips

Mondo grass can be used as a dense groundcover and for erosion control because it spreads by rhizomes. Use it for border edges and in containers.

Recommended

O. japonicus produces dark green, grass-like foliage that grows 8–14" long and forms an evergreen mat of lush foliage, resembling an unkempt lawn. Short spikes of white, occasionally lilac-tinged flowers emerge in summer, followed by metallic blue fruit. Many cultivars are available in dwarf or variegated forms. **'Nanus'** (dwarf mondo grass) grows only 2–6" tall and is slower growing than the standard species.

This plant is a member of the lily family and does not like being mowed. You can remove winter-damaged foliage before new growth emerges in spring.

O. planiscapus has two popular cultivars. **'Ebknizam'** ('Ebony Knight'; black mondo grass, black lily turf) has curving, almost black leaves and dark lavender flowers. It grows 4–6" tall and 6–12" wide. **'Nigrescens'** also has curving, almost black foliage, but its flowers are pink to white-flushed pink. It grows 6–12" tall and 12" wide. Both cultivars produce dark, berry-like fruit.

Features: groundcover habit; uniquely colored foliage; lavender, pink or white-flushed pink flowers **Height:** 2–12" **Spread:** 6–12" **Hardiness:** zones 5–9

Moneywort
Lysimachia

'Aurea' (above & below)

Moneywort is a lovely, low-growing, ground-covering perennial prized for its colorful foliage.

Growing
Moneywort grows well in **light shade** or **partial shade**. The soil should be of **average fertility, humus rich** and **moist**. Divide this plant in spring or fall. The trailing stems can be cut back if they begin to spread farther than you would like.

Try using moneywort in a bog-themed container.

Tips
An attractive and carefree addition to a moist border, moneywort is also a good plant to include in a rock garden, along a rock wall or in a container where the trailing stems have room to spread freely.

Recommended
L. nummularia is a prostrate, spreading plant with trailing stems. It bears bright yellow flowers in summer. A yellow-leaved cultivar called **'Aurea'** (golden creeping Jenny) is popular and is frequently available.

Also called: creeping Jenny **Features:** yellow flowers; attractive foliage **Height:** 2–4" **Spread:** 18" or more **Hardiness:** zones 2–8

Periwinkle

Vinca

Periwinkle is a dependable, spreading groundcover, and one plant can cover almost any size area. Its reliability and ease of growth are second to none.

Growing

Periwinkle grows best in **partial to full shade**, in **fertile, moist, well-drained** soil. It adapts to many types of soil, but it turns yellow if the soil is too dry or the sun is too hot.

Divide in early spring or fall, or whenever it becomes overgrown. If periwinkle begins to outgrow its space, it may be sheared back hard in early spring. The sheared-off ends may have rooted along the stems; these rooted cuttings may be transplanted or potted and given away as gifts.

Tips

Periwinkle is a useful and attractive groundcover in a shrub border, under trees or on a shady bank, and it prevents soil erosion. It is shallow rooted and able to outcompete weeds, but it won't interfere with deeper-rooted shrubs.

Recommended

V. major (greater periwinkle, large periwinkle) is an evergreen perennial that forms a mat of vigorous, upright to trailing stems 10–18" tall bearing dark green foliage. Purple to violet blue flowers are borne in a flush in spring and sporadically throughout summer. **'Variegata'** has leaves with creamy white edges. (Zones 6–9)

V. minor (above & below)

V. minor (creeping periwinkle, lesser periwinkle) forms a low, loose mat of trailing stems 4–8" tall. Purple or blue flowers are borne in a flush in spring and sporadically throughout summer. Many cultivars are available with different-colored flowers or variegated foliage. (Zones 4–8)

Creeping periwinkle is a great plant for use in mixed containers. As it drapes over the container edge, it dramatically enhances its companions.

Also called: vinca **Features:** trailing foliage; purple to violet blue flowers **Height:** 4–18" **Spread:** 18" to indefinite **Hardiness:** zones 4–9

Spotted Dead Nettle
Lamium

'White Nancy' (above), 'Beacon Silver' (below)

Spotted dead nettle is a splendid shade groundcover. In flower it is wonderful, but the key to its value is its weaving mounds of fabulously attractive, variegated foliage.

Growing
Spotted dead nettle prefers **partial shade** or **light shade** in **humus-rich, moist, well-drained** soil of **average fertility**. It is drought tolerant in the shade but can develop bare patches if the soil is allowed to dry out for extended periods. Divide and replant in fall if bare spots become unsightly.

Spotted dead nettle remains compact if sheared back after flowering. If it remains green over winter, shear it back in early spring.

Tips
This plant makes a useful groundcover for woodland or shade gardens. It works well under shrubs in a border, where it helps keep weeds down. Spotted dead nettle can also be used as a trailing plant in containers.

Recommended
L. maculatum is a low-growing, spreading species that has green leaves marked with white or silver. Many cultivars are available including the pink-flowering **'Pink Chablis.'**

Spotted dead nettle can become invasive in a garden if it is kept consistently moist.

Features: white, pink or red-purple, spring or summer flowers; decorative, often variegated foliage
Height: 8–10" **Spread:** 36" **Hardiness:** zones 3–8

Glossary

Acid soil: soil with a pH lower than 7.0

Annual: a plant that germinates, flowers, sets seed and dies in one growing season

Alkaline soil: soil with a pH higher than 7.0

Basal leaves: leaves that form from the crown, at the base of the plant

Bract: a modified leaf at the base of a flower or flower cluster

Corm: a bulblike, food-storing, underground stem, resembling a bulb without scales

Crown: the part of the plant at or just below soil level where the shoots join the roots

Cultivar: a cultivated plant variety with one or more distinct differences from the species, e.g., in flower color or disease resistance

Damping off: fungal disease causing seedlings to rot at soil level and topple over

Deadhead: to remove spent flowers to maintain a neat appearance and encourage a longer blooming season

Direct sow: to sow seeds directly in the garden

Dormancy: a period of plant inactivity, usually during winter or unfavorable conditions

Double flower: a flower with an unusually large number of petals

Genus: a category of biological classification between the species and family levels; the first word in a scientific name indicates the genus

Grafting: a type of propagation in which a stem or bud of one plant is joined onto the rootstock of another plant of a closely related species

Hardy: capable of surviving unfavorable conditions, such as cold weather or frost, without protection

Hip: the fruit of a rose, containing the seeds

Humus: decomposed or decomposing organic material in the soil

Hybrid: a plant resulting from natural or human-induced cross-breeding between varieties, species or genera

Inflorescence: a flower cluster

Neutral soil: soil with a pH of 7.0

Perennial: a plant that takes three or more years to complete its life cycle

pH: a measure of acidity or alkalinity; the soil pH influences availability of nutrients for plants

Rhizome: a root-like, food-storing stem that grows horizontally at or just below soil level, from which new shoots may emerge

Rootball: the root mass and surrounding soil of a plant

Seedhead: dried, inedible fruit that contains seeds; the fruiting stage of the inflorescense

Self-seeding: reproducing by means of seeds without human assistance, so that new plants constantly replace those that die

Semi-double flower: a flower with petals in two or three rings

Single flower: a flower with a single ring of typically four or five petals

Species: the fundamental unit of biological classification; the entity from which cultivars and varieties are derived

Standard: a shrub or small tree grown with an erect main stem, accomplished either through pruning and training or by grafting the plant onto a tall, straight stock

Sucker: a shoot that comes up from the root, often some distance from the plant; it can be separated to form a new plant once it develops its own roots

Tender: incapable of surviving the climatic conditions of a given region and requiring protection from frost or cold

Tuber: the thick section of a rhizome bearing nodes and buds

Variegation: foliage that has more than one color, often patched or striped or bearing leaf margins of a different color

Variety: a naturally occurring variant of a species

Index of Common Names and Genera